Introducing the Second Edition of

Cooking with Chef Brad
Those Wonderful Grains!
Series

Special Features:

- Reformatted cover and layout
- Simplified instructions
- Enhanced recipes using **Those Wonderful Grains!**
- Additional recommended ingredient substitutions
- Additional tips and updated information

Cooking with Chef Brad
Those Wonderful Grains!

Cooking with Chef Brad
Those Wonderful Grains II

Cooking with Chef Brad
Favorite Pressure Cooker Recipes

Cooking with Chef Brad
Whole Grain Comfort Foods

Conveniently order online
www.chefbrad.com

Cooking with Chef Brad

Those Wonderful Grains II

By Brad E Petersen
"Chef Brad"

Second Edition

MemoryMaker Productions
Grass Valley, California

MemoryMaker Productions
P.O. Box 2524
Grass Valley, CA 95945-2524

Cooking with Chef Brad
Those Wonderful Grains II

© 2011 by Brad E Petersen
All rights reserved. No part of this work
covered by copyright may be
used, reproduced, stored in a retrieval
system, or transmitted in any form or by
any means, electronic, mechanical, photocopying,
recording, or otherwise without the prior written
permission of the copyright holder, except brief
quotations used in a review.

Notice: The purpose of this book is to educate and
entertain. The author and MemoryMaker
Productions shall have neither liability nor
responsibility to any person or entity with
respect to any loss or damage caused, or
alleged to have been caused, directly or
indirectly, by the information contained in this
book.

First edition published 2003
Second edition published 2011
Printed in Hong Kong
2011-A-BB

ISBN: 978-1-936992-07-2

For questions about ingredients and
recipes, check Chef Brad's website:
www.chefbrad.com
or email chef@chefbrad.com

Cover design: Jennco Executive Services and Marianne McKnight
Cover photo: Wendi Lee Photography, Inc.
Chef's hat design: Gloria Armstrong

Dedication

*To my wife, Louise,
who has given all,
heart, soul, and health,
to let me live my dream.
Words are not enough to express
the feelings I have in my heart
for her.*

Who is Chef Brad?

Chef Brad Petersen is a native of Arizona. His career in the food business began early in life. By age nine he was doing the majority of the cooking for his family. By age thirteen he was working as a busboy, and by age eighteen he was comfortable in all areas of the food and beverage industry. He served a two-year L.D.S. mission to the Caribbean when he was nineteen. He loved the food there and spent as much time as possible learning the local recipes. He eventually relocated to Mesa Arizona, where he jumped right back into the restaurant business; from waiting on tables, to cooking, to management—he's done it all.

Chef Brad has owned a catering business, a consulting business, a kitchen store, and his own very successful café, where of course he served dishes using grains. Over the years he has gained an excellent reputation as a chef; his food is unique and fresh. He has devoted the last fifteen years to studying grains, his greatest love, and has developed and written four cookbooks featuring "Those Wonderful Grains." He has a passion for teaching and education. He has developed a wonderful following and is respected for his gift of making healthful food taste great and inspiring others to eat better and enjoy time spent in the kitchen.

Currently he has his own cooking show, "Fusion Grain Cooking," that airs on BYU TV, and works for Thermador Appliances as a national spokesperson and executive chef. He operates an expanding internet site and travels across the country teaching about nutrition and health. A gifted teacher, he is passionate, full of energy, and loves people. He believes in creating "Fond Food Memories" whenever possible.

His love for grains and food has made Chef Brad a leading authority in America on grains and the history of grains. He believes strongly that America is ready for a change and is starving for knowledge on how to eat better and be healthier.

Acknowledgment

How can I ever thank all those wonderful, supportive friends who have stood by me and believed in what I am doing—and who have eaten everything I have made with gusto. I am so grateful for the years of teaching and for the support I've received from class members and loyal "Chef Brad" fans.

I am grateful to my best friends—Keith Smith, Jordan Clark, Michael Bigler, and Heath Lindsey—for the constant belief and support that they have given me through thick and thin. I love to cook for these guys because they love it all—and if they don't, they tell me the truth.

If everyone could have the publisher that I have—Marianne McKnight is the best, constant in her encouragement and dedicated to perfection. I adore her and am so grateful for her efforts past, present, and future. My thanks also to Ralph McKnight, the genius behind the recipe database that made this cookbook possible.

While writing this book, I had the distinct privilege of having my office in the home of my father-in-law, George Wilson. What a great blessing this was for me to have his support and vast wisdom. He had the responsibility of listening to my ravings and ranting, sometimes late into the night. He has since passed away but how I love that man and have appreciated his love and support.

Last of all, but most importantly, is my family. What is man without his family? Building family ties that will last forever—that's what life is all about. We have built many in the kitchen and will continue to create more great "fond food memories" in the years to come.

My family has been wonderful on this journey of discovery. They have patiently sampled all kinds of foods. Not all my creations have been good, but I still remain the best in their eyes. When it all comes right down to it, if *they* think I am the best chef in the world, then that is all that really matters.

Family is wonderful—from spouse to children, brothers, sisters, in-laws, aunts, and uncles, to nieces and nephews, and, of course, parents. Family is where we receive the most support and love that helps us to reach for the stars.

I love you all. Thank you for everything.

Chef Brad

Table of Contents

Introduction 1
   Ingredients 4
   Equipment 5
   Resource 7

Those Wonderful Grains 9
   Amaranth 11
   Barley 13
   Buckwheat 14
   Bulgar Wheat 16
   Corn/Popcorn 17
   Farro 19
   Kamut® 20
   Millet 22
   Oat Groats 24
   Quinoa 26
   Quinoa, Red 28
   Rice, Long Grain, Brown 29
   Rye 30
   Spelt 31
   Teff 33
   Triticale 34
   Wheat 35
   Grains Cooking Chart 36
   Grains Usage Chart 38

Recipes 41
   Breads 41
   Breakfast Foods 73
   Salads & Dressings 107
   Soups, Stews, & Main Dishes 143
   Desserts 169

Index 181

Introduction

I cannot believe that I have written another cookbook. This is so exciting! After years of using my first cookbook, Cooking with Chef Brad, Those Wonderful Grains!, I still love it. When I wrote it, I was just beginning my journey into the Wonderful World of Grains, a journey that I have enjoyed over the past several years. It has been wonderful to travel and teach and develop new and exciting recipes. I have learned so much! In order to share what I've learned I wrote this book, Those Wonderful Grains II. There is so much more to learn, of course. In some ways, in fact, I feel that I have just begun to learn, and I get so excited just thinking about where we are going and what will happen next.

Over the years I have learned some very important things with regard to grains and how to use them in the foods that we eat. I've enjoying sharing this knowledge with others. I had been teaching a long time, however, before one day I realized that I was not making much sense to anyone. I mean, people loved the concept of healthful eating habits, but that was about it. They needed more practical help on how to make it work for them. I determined to find a better way to get my message across.

Grains are so important to our diet. The reason is very basic: They contain all we need for good health and nutrition. Additionally, they taste great. What could be better—great-tasting nutrition that we could use every day.

The problem was that the idea of improving our eating habits just seemed too hard. We are all so busy and society has trained us to rely on cold cereals and fast prepared foods that can be put in the microwave and eaten. We want it easy or we won't do it. We want to be healthy but without any effort. We want instant gratification, instant results.

As I've searched for the answer to motivating people to adopt a healthier lifestyle, I've noticed that many live under the false myth that healthful food cannot taste good. If you lived through the '70s and '80s, that is where that concept came from. Healthful food did not taste good back then; in fact, it was nasty. No wonder we are afraid of health food. Maybe we need to change the name to something other than health food or teach the rising generation what good health food is, then maybe in a few years the bad memories of the '70s and '80s will vanish.

I have observed other interesting things about people. We all want to be healthy and most of us are hungry for a better way. We are tired of fad diets where we end up worse than when we started. We are tired of the sensationalism of the '90s and we are tired of spending lots of time in the kitchen without results. We all want help, we want to fix healthful food, we want to feel better, we want our families to eat better, and we want practical advice that works—and without a whole lot of fuss and bother. The good news is that if you are reading this, you are on the right track to starting better habits.

So then I got really excited about exploring a better way of sharing what I've learned, and this is what I discovered: It all has to do with eating more grains. When we do we add much needed fiber to our diets. I am convinced that almost all of today's health problems have to do with poor eating habits. Eating grains on a regular basis can and will change everything about our lives. This is not a fad diet; this is a practical, commonsense way of life that has proven successful time and time again. I am excited to share some of the secrets to improved health that I have learned in this book.

I will also share some great recipes, but right now I will give you the most important recipe of all. It is simply this: Add grains to all the things you are cooking right now. You don't have to re-create, just add them to what you have already created. Grains—and beans too—are great in salads, soups, casseroles, baked goods, and just about anything else. Just ask my family—I add them to about everything we eat.

And it's really not that hard. You just need to prepare the grains and beans ahead of time and have them on hand in order to maximize your use of these powerhouses of nutrition. For example, if you have a couple of cups of beans or grains already cooked up, it is easy just to add them in or put them on top of whatever you are cooking. It's a great way to add nutrition to your diet, and it really does work. Mind you, it is usually better to start out slowly and add a little bit at a time. We must always remember, no matter how healthful it is, if no one will eat it, we have wasted our time.

I have a passion for using grains and beans in food that I prepare. My family has gotten used to it and actually loves many of the things I prepare. It didn't happen overnight; it was a process. We added a little bit here and a little more there until we found our comfort zone. I have learned what I can and cannot do, and I try not to make a big deal over it; I just cook and camouflage as much as possible. And remember, if at first you don't succeed, don't give up. Just try another grain or bean and another recipe, and eventually you will succeed. Success is great.So, enjoy this book. I am sure there are more books to come, for I have just started my journey of discovery into *Those Wonderful Grains!* I hope you join me.

Ingredients

Quality ingredients are essential to a successful end result. Since this is a book about grains, I will start with them. All grains are not created equal. I only use certified chemical-free or organic grains in my recipes. These are grown by higher standards and by people who are committed to quality.

I have searched for a long time to find a grains supplier that shares my passion for quality. I finally found that company! I have teamed up with West Mountain Farms from Spanish Fork, Utah, to provide you with the best quality of grains that can be found. We supply flours that are chemical and bromine free. Bromines, chemicals found in most refined flours, are toxic to the human body. Recent research has shown that many people who have a wheat allergy are really fighting the toxins in the grains. That is why I recommend using the flours that are bromine free.

I am passionate about finding quality products and ingredients when cooking. From herbs to spices, soup bases to oils and vinegars, I try to find the best quality. If you are going to go to the effort of cooking, use quality ingredients. That is what makes the difference between a mediocre cook and a gourmet cook. Quality does count.

If products are mentioned in this book that you are unable to find, replace them with ones that you love.

Equipment

Anyone can bake or cook with the proper equipment, quality ingredients, and great recipes. This book contains great recipes; the results, however, will depend on quality ingredients and equipment. It is amazing what happens in the kitchen when we have the right equipment to do the job. Kitchen work is hard and demanding. One of the ways to make it less of a chore is to have proper equipment.

I had a customer come into my store a few years ago with his wife. It was wonderful. He just kept pointing at things, saying, "I want this and I want that for my wife." She just smiled as he bought all of the best equipment I had. I asked what the special occasion was. He said, and I will never forget it, "I was at work the other day, and I realized that I had everything I needed to accomplish my job—all state-of-the-art equipment. I realized that my wife deserved the same consideration to accomplish her job at home, so here we are." You should have seen her face. That was one happy woman, and I am sure he reaped the reward of making sure she had what she needed to cook meals for her family.

Cooking for a family is a full-time, demanding job that requires effort, time, and planning to create meals that taste good and are good for you. Make it less of a chore by having whatever you need to bake, cook, and create food for those you love.

When buying equipment one of the most important things to remember is to buy quality. Quality lasts and makes the job more pleasant. Long term we spend less when we buy quality. I learned the hard way, after throwing away cheap pots and pans and kitchen gadgets—and throwing away ruined food that did not turn out right because of the poor equipment I had used to prepare it. Many times we cook with faulty equipment and place the blame on ourselves for not being able to cook. I have found that most anyone can prepare great food if they use quality equipment and ingredients.

Those Wonderful Grains II

I feel that there are a few pieces of equipment that are absolutely necessary to prepare great, healthful food:

Bread Mixer
A good bread mixer is so important for homemade baked goods. I prefer Bosch-style kitchen machines for their ease and durability when making great whole grain breads and baked goods, and the Bosch blender is great for blender pancakes.

Pressure Cooker
A good pressure cooker is essential to cooking grains and beans with ease. Pressure cooking has greatly improved over the last few years; there is no longer the fear of the pressure cooker blowing up.

Grain Mill
A grain mill is one of the best investments for health and nutrition if you are going to start using whole grains. Nothing can compare to the ease of grinding grains right in your own kitchen, not to overlook the tremendous health benefits derived from freshly ground grains. I love the WonderMill™ and the Nutra-Mill™. Both are great mills, quiet and clean, and they'll last forever.

Blender
A good blender is a must in the kitchen. Most cheap blenders will not do what we want them to do. To make blender pancakes, you will need a powerful blender that can grind the grains effectively. I love the blender that comes with the Bosch, but I also adore other high-power blenders. They are really wonderful.

Quality Cookware
Quality cookware makes the difference between most failures and successes in cooking. From bread pans to sauté pans and everything in-between, buy quality. Quality cookware will last for years, and you will love the end results. If you are going to spend a great deal of time in the kitchen, do all you can to ensure that the end result is as good as it can be.

Gadgets

Gadgets can be fun and make the job easier. From salad spinners to garlic presses, gadgets make cooking fun and exciting. One of the worst things to do, however, is to buy junkie ones. Most people have drawers full of useless gadgets. Never buy a gadget on an impulse, and when you do buy one, buy quality.

Resource

For the latest information about products and ingredients for your kitchen, go to www.chefbrad.com. If you have questions about specific recipes or ingredients, email me at chef@chefbrad.com.

Notes

Those Wonderful Grains!

Amaranth

Amaranth is a "new" name, but the grain itself is ancient. A 500-year-old seed, amaranth to the Aztecs meant great and mystical things. They believed that a single spoonful could turn a wimpy man into an Incredible Hulk, and eating a steady diet of amaranth could produce a race of Supermen.

Not only was amaranth grown to be given to the emperor Montezuma by the tons, it was also used for religious practices. It was a source of energy and fortitude and was as important to the Aztecs as the corn and beans that kept them alive.

Montezuma and the Aztecs' "amaranth" practice came to an end when Hernando Cortez observed their doings. He was so offended that he had every field of blooming amaranth burned—from the Gulf of California to the Bay of Campeche. Not only did he burn the amaranth but those caught using it had their hands cut off. With the pillage of the amaranth fields, historians say, came the end of the Aztec empire. Stripped and deprived of their "power food," warriors were left dispirited, with nothing more to do but become peasants without a leader or a focus.

Even though Hernando Cortez returned to Spain with a sense of victory for terminating the Aztecs and this wonderful grain, he did not completely win. Today, half a millennium later, we are rediscovering its healthful and tonic affects on the body.

I adore this wonderful small, yet powerful, grain. Gluten-free, it can be ground into flour, which can be used for almost anything, from thickening sauces to cooking for breakfast. You will delight in the lightness of this flour; it's nutty but the mild flavor is neither offensive nor overpowering. Amaranth is considered a perfect baby food, as it is easily digested and is packed with essential amino acids.

Although I enjoy using the flour, I think this grain really comes to life when popped. I love the wonderful flavor of popped amaranth. It is reported to give bread a lighter texture, an extra bonus, and can be added to anything, from breads to candies. I especially like to use it in cookies and breads. For hot cereal I use the

Those Wonderful Grains II

flour with the ratio of one part water to five parts flour, and then I sprinkle popped amaranth on top for extra flavor. I often garnish a spinach salad with popped amaranth.

Had Hernando Cortez only known about the wonderful flavor and exceptional health benefits of this great grain, history just might have been written differently.

Amaranth Popping Instructions: Use a deep pot with no oil. Just heat the pot and to see if the pot is hot enough, place in a pinch of amaranth. If it pops, then you are ready to go. Add no more than two tablespoons at once; adding more will cause this delicately small grain to burn. One-quarter cup of grain will yield a cup of popped amaranth.

Nutrient content per 1/2 cup cooked amaranth:

364 calories	148 mg calcium	7 g dietary fiber	1.3 mg niacin
14 g protein	443 mg phosp.	0 RE vitamin A	356 mg potassium
6 g fat	7.4 mg iron	.08 mg thiamin	65 g carbohydrate
1 g saturated fat	21 mg sodium	.20 mg riboflavin	
0 mg cholesterol		4 mg vitamin C	

Barley

We know that garlic, onion, and tea are common antitoxins when a cold occurs, but did you know that barley can help with a cold as well? It has large amounts of protein, niacin, thiamine, and potassium. A cup of barley soup will be sure to set you vertical.

Barley is a comfort food that can fill you up and delay feelings of hunger. The advantage of this is appetite control! Barley cereal is one of the first solid foods recommended for babies. It is one of the richest sources of both soluble and insoluble fiber.

Barley has components that can inhibit fat and cholesterol absorption in the intestine. This results in lower blood cholesterol, especially LDL (harmful) cholesterol, in people with high cholesterol. Barley is low in gluten, though not gluten free.

Its most common form is pearled barley. It adds a delicious dimension to your foods. Try barley in your favorite recipes! It cooks up so easily.

Barley has been around for thousands of years. The first documented sign of barley was in 1520 BC with the Chinese. Later, it was discovered that Asia had been growing and harvesting barley as well. Barley was the staple food of the Roman gladiators and one of the earliest cereal foods used by man.

As you see, it is by no accident that we love barley soup. It is a comfort food because it gives us so much of what we need to sustain health. One of the greatest misfortunes is that we only use barley for soup. It has so many other great uses.

Nutrient content per 1 cup cooked pearl barley:

193 calories	17 mg calcium	9 g dietary fiber	0 mg vitamin C
4 g protein	85 mg phosph.	1 RE vitamin A	3.2 mg niacin
1 g fat, 0 sat. fat	2.1 mg iron	.13 mg thiamin	146 mg potassium
0 mg cholesterol	5 mg sodium	.10 mg riboflavin	44 g carbohydrate

Buckwheat/Kasha

The proteins in buckwheat are the best known source of complex carbohydrates. Buckwheat contains a high proportion of all eight amino acids, which the body does not manufacture but are nonetheless deemed absolutely essential for keeping it in tiptop shape. Buckwheat is closer to being a complete protein than any other plant source, even better than soybeans.

Buckwheat is no relation to wheat. In fact, it is a cousin to the rhubarb plant. Gluten free, it is a great substitute flour for things like pancakes. I appreciate this wonderful grain for its strong, earthy flavor, not to mention its nutritional value.

Its most common use is for buckwheat pancakes, a favorite in the South and fast becoming a favorite all over because of the great nutrition and fiber content. I also often add the flour to pizza dough and french breads. I like the rustic flavor and look that it adds.

Buckwheat comes in three flavors. I say flavors because each one has a distinct difference. The first is regular buckwheat; it is the whole buckwheat with the hull on. It has an almost black appearance. This form is best used as flour, which can be used in almost anything calling for flour. It does not have gluten, so it can not be used to make bread on its own.

The second form is hulled buckwheat, or some people call it kasha. It has the hull removed. This one has the mildest flavor of the three. It works well steamed up and used as a side dish or in salads. I use it side by side with eggplant in Italian dishes but have used it in many other dishes with great results. It does well in soups and the flour is excellent to use. If you are not used to small black objects in your food, then the hulled buckwheat flour is perfect. You will get the flavor but not the overwhelming black hulls.

THOSE WONDERFUL GRAINS!

The third flavor is called roasted kasha. It is the hulled kasha roasted to bring out the flavor. It has a strong flavor, very earthy. This one is used mostly in salads and side dishes. You need to make the choice; I prefer the hulled, unroasted kind for side dishes and salads and the whole buckwheat for flour. Whatever your choice, you will love the earthy flavor and high level of nutrition of this wonderful, unique grain.

Nutrient content per 1 cup cooked buckwheat:
182 calories	138 mg phosph.	1.6 mg iron	.08 mg riboflavin
7 g protein	39 g carbohydrate	8 mg sodium	1.9 mg niacin
1 g fat, 0 sat.	14 mg calcium	174 mg potassium	0 mg vitamin C
0 mg cholesterol	6 g dietary fiber	.08 mg thiamin	0 RE vitamin A

Nutrient content per 1 cup cooked kasha (roasted buckwheat):
182 calories	138 mg phosph.	1.6 mg iron	.08 mg riboflavin
7 g protein	39 g carbohydrate	8 mg sodium	1.9 mg niacin
1 g fat, 0 sat.	14 mg calcium	174 mg potassium	0 mg vitamin C
0 mg cholesterol	5 g dietary fiber	.08 mg thiamin	0 RE vitamin A

Bulgur Wheat

This amazing grain has so many wonderful characteristics that I do not know where to begin. Bulgur could perhaps be the first processed food. It dates back to 2800 BC. Its mention has been recorded in the history of ancient Babylonians and Hebrew populations some four thousand years ago. Roman, Israeli, Egyptian, and Arab civilizations recorded eating dried cooked wheat as early as 1000 BC. Bulgur has many names, from "cerealis" by the Romans, "dagan" by the Israelites, and "arisah" by other Middle Easterners. Whatever the name, it is basically the same thing—soaked or cooked whole wheat that is then sun dried, cracked, and then sifted for different sizes that are in turn used for different purposes.

This grain has been called "the perfect food for the new millennium." In contrast to whole wheat, bulgur can be prepared very quickly and be ready to eat with minimal preparation; this is one of its main benefits. It requires little fuel, which in many countries is still an issue.

Bulgur also stores extremely well and is packed with all kinds of minerals and nutrients. It is a great substitute for converted rice and can be used in many things. It is easier to digest and has a wonderful nutty flavor. It is excellent as a meat extender or as a meat substitute in vegetarian dishes. I use it in salads, and it is perfect cooked and added to breads for a chewy, wonderful texture.

Nutrient content per 3/4 c. cooked bulgur wheat:
151 calories   4 g fat, 1 g sat. fat   0 mg cholesterol   300 mg sodium
27 g carbohyd.   7 g dietary fiber   4 g protein

Corn/Popcorn

Corn and popcorn are members of the grass family of plants. Corn is a native grain of the American continents. The Mayan, Aztec, and Inca Indians first grew it more than fifty-six hundred years ago. The Indians used it for many things, from the sugar-filled leaves as chewing gum to the young corn as a fresh vegetable. The dry corn was ground into flour. The Native American Indians included corn in the "Three Sisters"—corn, squash, and beans—important sources of food and planted together.

Popcorn was used as a food as well as decoration. Necklaces were made from popcorn. When Columbus came, Indians wearing necklaces of popcorn greeted him and presented him with baskets of popped corn. Some of the first popcorn was popped right on the oiled husk and eaten off the same. The early pilgrims ate popcorn at the first Thanksgiving dinner.

The early pilgrims might have died during the first winter in America had not the Native Americans showed them how to use corn, a wonderful grain. They taught the pilgrims how to use it in soups, bread, puddings, fried corn cakes, and much more. They even taught the early Americans how to plant the corn, placing kernels in the ground along with a small fish that acted as fertilizer. Corn was so valuable to the early settlers that they used corn to trade for furs and food.

Corn has long been a staple in the American diet, and it did not take long for the rest of the world to catch on. Corn is the most widely distributed crop in the world. It can grow virtually anywhere under almost any circumstance.

Popcorn has less starch than corn, and I enjoy using it in baking. I love the results of corn bread made with popcorn. Popcorn is a great treat that is also very good for you. It can be a great dieting aid. Eaten immediately before a meal, it will take the edge off an appetite.

Those Wonderful Grains II

It has excellent dietary fiber and roughage that compares to bran flakes. The uses of both popcorn and corn are endless. From necklaces to microwave heating pads, corn is truly a wonderful American grain.

Nutrient content per 1 cup popcorn (air-popped, unsalted, and unbuttered):

31 calories	1 mg calcium	1 g dietary fiber	0 mg vitamin C
1 g protein	24 mg phosp.	2 RE vitamin A	.2 mg niacin
0 g fat, 0 sat. fat	.2 mg iron	.02 mg thiamin	24 mg potassium
0 mg cholesterol	0 mg sodium	.02 mg riboflavin	6 g carbohydrate

Farro

Farro (pronounced FAHR-oh) is not wheat but a plant and grain in its own right. For centuries it has been a mainstay of Tuscany, in northeastern Italy. Pushed aside in recent decades by easier-to-grow-and-harvest varieties of common wheat, farro is making a comeback among health-conscious cooks and consumers.

A farro grain looks like light brown rice and has a nutty taste. Unlike wheat, the farro husk adheres to the grain, just as in barley and oats. Its fiber content is, therefore, high and so are its nutrients. It is packed with minerals and nutrients as well as oils, which enhance its fibrous properties. Specifically, farro is loaded with vitamin E, which acts as an antioxidant and is key in fighting disease and staying healthy. It is also rich in fiber and magnesium, as well as vitamins A, B, and C. Protein content is high and when combined with legumes, it forms a complete protein source.

About ninety percent of people allergic to hybridized wheat can tolerate farro products. Farro has a different genetic makeup than hybridized wheat, and its gluten is more easily digested.

This wonderful grain from Italy will steal your heart away with its truly excellent flavor and texture. This grain is great as a side dish and more especially as an addition to rustic-style homemade grains. It is easy to cook and stores well in the refrigerator, making it the perfect addition to salads and other dishes.

In Italy it is used as a pasta wheat. It works well for pasta but don't stop there. The flour is wonderful in any baked goods and takes the place of white flour in baking. Farro is not used alone in making bread; rather add it to bread dough as a flour or, as I prefer, steamed then added whole. It gives breads a wonderful, chewy texture. It looks like barley when cooked, but if you are not a barley fan, don't let that keep you away. The flavor and texture, I am sure, will delight and satisfy you.

Nutrient content per 3/4 c. cooked farro:
279 calories   11 g fat, 3 g sat. fat   10 mg cholesterol   363 mg sodium
367 g carbohyd.   4 g dietary fiber   10 g protein

Kamut®

Kamut® came to us from Egypt. It is a type of wheat and can be substituted for any wheat varieties, but it has shown to be superior both in taste and nutrition. Kamut® wheat has a wonderful buttery flavor and great texture. It contains no cholesterol and is easily digestible.

Additionally, of special interest to those suffering from wheat allergies or sensitivities, research has shown that many who cannot tolerate wheat can handle Kamut®. In a recent study, seventy percent of those tested showed a reaction to common wheat rather than the Kamut® wheat.

The most striking superiority quality of Kamut® is found in its protein level, up to forty percent higher than the national average for wheat. Compared to wheat, it is higher in eight out of nine minerals, including magnesium and zinc. It contains more of the natural antioxidant selenium, has thirty percent more vitamin E and up to sixty-five percent more amino acids, and boasts more lipids and fatty acids. Because of its higher percentage of lipids, which produce more energy than carbohydrates, Kamut® can be described as a "high energy grain." Athletes, people with busy lives, and anyone looking for quality nutrition will find Kamut® a valuable addition to their diet.

This is truly a wonderful grain. I remember first hearing about a grain that made great pancakes and waffles. So began my love affair with Kamut®. It does make the most wonderful pancakes and waffles—but why stop there? I often use it in baking. From banana breads to coffee cakes, this grain brings out the best in flavor and texture. It is so buttery; you will love the flavor. I also use this grain cooked whole in salads, stews, and side dishes. It has a chewy quality that I relish. It also makes the very best cracked cereal I have ever eaten. It is easy to digest and is big on flavor.

To summarize, Kamut® is delicious and diverse. You can use it in many types of foods, like cereals, soups, breads, cookies, snacks, waffles, baked goods, main dishes, and more. It has a wonderful sweet flavor and can be substituted for many wheat varieties. Give this delicious grain a try and improve your daily consumption of protein and many other vitamins and minerals.

Nutrient content per 1 cup cooked Kamut®:
258 calories	18 mg sodium	10 g protein	4 g dietary fiber
3 g fat	44 g carbohydrate

Millet

Millet has found its way to North America from northern China, where it originated in 618–907 AD. Back then, China was divided between the north and south according to the principal grain grown in that region. Throughout time rice moved from the south to the north and began to be used by the whole country. Millet, on the other hand, moved on to other parts of the world. For instance, millet flourished in the Roman Empire and was the main cereal in the Middle Ages.

Because of millet's drought-resistant tendencies, it has thrived in semi-arid conditions in areas of our country, including Kansas, Colorado, and North Dakota. This grain can be planted late and still mature in time for a fall harvest. Many farmers whose corn or wheat crop was destroyed will quickly plant millet. In addition, millet does not strip the soil of its nutrients as does wheat, which means millet can be planted three years in succession. This makes millet extremely plentiful and useful.

Not only is millet useful, it also has other wonderful characteristics. For instance, this tiny seed has the most complete protein and the most iron of any of the other true cereal grains. It is gluten free and rich in phosphorus, amino acids, and B vitamins. Because of its high alkaline ash content, this grain is easily digestible.

Millet also has a sweet and light nature. When cooked with little water, millet is light and fluffy. Add more water and it becomes mushy like polenta or mashed potatoes. Millet is a wonderful grain and has shown to be helpful and plentiful in times of need.

Interestingly enough, two-thirds of the world population depends on millet, while here in the United States we grow most of our millet to feed to our birds and livestock. It is a great substitute for white rice. Because of its ease in cooking, millet makes a great side dish and breakfast dish. I will often substitute it for rice in Spanish rice dishes or other recipes that call for white rice. Millet is also highly recommended for babies and small children because of the high nutrition and digestibility.

Those Wonderful Grains!

Millet is considered by some to be the most versatile grain in the world. Try adding it to just about anything and discover why most of the world loves this grain and what we are missing out on in the United States.

Nutrient content per 1 cup boiled millet:

284 calories	7 mg calcium	3 g dietary fiber	0 mg vitamin C
8 g protein	240 mg phosp.	0 RE vitamin A	3.2 mg niacin
2 g fat, 0 sat. fat	1.5 mg iron	.25 mg thiamin	149 mg potassium
0 mg cholesterol	5 mg sodium	.20 mg riboflavin	57 g carbohydrate

Oats

As many of us know, eating oats is an excellent way to lower blood cholesterol. But did you also know that eating a healthful diet of oats can reduce the risk of heart disease, cancer, and diabetes?

Oats have been around for so long there isn't any record of a first appearance. There are records, though, dating back to the fifth century AD, when the Romans discovered that Attila the Hun fed his barbarian troops oats, which turned them into fierce tigers. It never reached the tables of the upper class, however. This grain remained mainly as food for the poor. It wasn't until the Crusaders' use of the grain that oats gained a respectable reputation. It was easy to carry and provided the strength needed to complete a long day's work. On returning home, the Crusaders planted fields in their native lands—Scotland, Ireland, Wales, England, Denmark, Germany, and France—where it is grown to this very day.

Today, oats are steadily gaining favor in the eyes of the health-conscious. Oats are a wonderful source of complex carbohydrates and are low in fat and are cholesterol free. They are a good source of fiber, both soluble and insoluble, and B vitamins. Oats are also easily digested and are a great source of protein. With a little bit of sugar, cream and butter, who wouldn't enjoy a bowl of oats every morning? What a wonderful idea!

Whole oat groats are oats that have had the hulls removed and have been heat-treated to stabilize enzymes, which cause rancidity. The groat actually is the basis for all cereal variations on the market. Oat groats can be prepared in many different forms: cereals, flour for breads, cookies, salads, and many more. Steel cut oat groats are whole oat groats that have each been cut into two or four pieces.

Those Wonderful Grains!

Oat groats make a great flour, which can be used in almost all baking, adding nutrition and taste. Even cooked up as a side dish, oats can be extremely tasty. I love the buttery texture, not to mention the outstanding nutrition gleaned from this underrated grain. Oats are a wise choice and will continue to be a wonderful way to stay healthy and to live longer.

Nutrient content per 1 cup cooked oat bran:

88 calories	22 mg calcium	7 g dietary fiber	0 mg vitamin C
7 g protein	261 mg phosp.	0 RE vitamin A	.3 mg niacin
2 g fat, 0 sat. fat	1.9 mg iron	.35 mg thiamin	201 mg potassium
0 mg cholesterol	2 mg sodium	.07 mg riboflavin	25 g carbohydrate

Nutrient content per 1 cup cooked oatmeal:

145 calories	19 mg calcium	5 g dietary fiber	0 mg vitamin C
6 g protein	177 mg phosp.	5 RE vitamin A	.3 mg niacin
2 g fat, 0 sat. fat	1.6 mg iron	.26 mg thiamin	131 mg potassium
0 mg cholesterol	2 mg sodium	.05 mg riboflavin	25 g carbohydrate

Quinoa

There is more to quinoa than just the funny name. Quinoa has been named the "super grain" by nutritionists because of its amazing and "super" qualities. Dating back to 3000 BC, this seed has been a vital part of the Andean diet. It was used in baking as well as in many other dishes eaten by the Andeans. Over the years quinoa has gone from being a wonderful, powerful, and desirable food to being poor and unwanted. As a result of the rise of the Spanish, other grains were introduced and grown, overtaking quinoa. The number of acres planted with this grain has plummeted drastically, from 111,000 acres to 32,000 acres in thirty years.

Quinoa has yet to be defeated, however. In the last ten years there has been an increasing interest in this grain—not only because of its quick cooking time and incredible ability to be substituted for protein-rich foods, such as cheese or beef, but also because of its nutritional value.

It is considered to have more than three times as much calcium and twice as much phosphorus as wheat. Plus, it contains equal, if not more, amounts of protein than powdered milk. Studies have shown that pregnant women who have a regular diet of quinoa can improve their milk secretion.

Quinoa is said to be the most complete food; it furnishes us with all the essential nutrients for living. It's no wonder that the Andeans found it to be their "Mother Grain." It truly does contribute to the healthy lifestyle we are all striving for.

This is a remarkable grain. It is so satisfying and easy to cook. It comes in three flavors or varieties—white, black, and red. I adore each one for different reasons.

I started cooking with white quinoa since it was the first one introduced into the United States. White quinoa is so versatile. One of the easiest ways to prepare it is to just mix it with rice. It sort of disappears into the rice, making it perfect for "sneak nutrition." It is amazing in soups, especially chicken noodle soup. I love this grain and continue to use it frequently.

Black quinoa is very high in lysine. I use the black variety for its texture and for the color contrast that it gives the foods. It cooks just like white rice and makes a great addition to rice. It is perfect in salads, and I also use it in soups and casseroles.

I cannot say enough good about this wonder grain. It's perfect in every way. I am so thrilled that we have it available today. What a great product we have now that greatly enhances the flavor and nutrition in our diet. To learn more about red quinoa, read the next section entitled "Quinoa, Red."

Nutrient content per 1/2 cup dry quinoa:

318 calories	51 mg calcium	4 g dietary fiber	0 mg vitamin C
11 g protein	349 mg phosp.	0 RE vitamin A	2.5 mg niacin
5 g fat, 1 sat. fat	7.9 mg iron	.17 mg thiamin	629 mg potassium
0 mg cholesterol	18 mg sodium	.34 mg riboflavin	59 g carbohydrate

Quinoa, Red

One of my personal favorites, red quinoa is the super grain from South America. Bolivia and Peru are the growers of this incredible grain. Ancient red quinoa is one of the most exciting grains to appear in years. Easy, quick, nutritious, and with a striking appearance, red quinoa is garnering rave reviews by professional chefs and home cooks everywhere.

Grown and harvested by the direct descendants of the original Incas, red quinoa is hand-tended from planting to final harvest in the ancient and traditional methods that date back hundreds of years.

I love red quinoa for its unique flavor and texture. It has a nutty flavor and the texture is pleasant. It is very appealing in looks before and after cooking. It cooks just like white rice and can be added to almost anything.

My very favorite breakfast is a big bowl of steamed or cooked red quinoa with a dash of sugar; combined with fresh fruits like peaches, bananas, or strawberries cut up; and topped off with a little bit of half & half. Talk about a wonderful experience! It does not get better than this.

Quinoa contains more high quality proteins than any other grain. It is called by the National Academy of Sciences as "one of the best sources of protein in the vegetable kingdom." It also contains all the essential amino acids in a balanced pattern. Quinoa is gluten free, making it perfect for people with gluten allergies.

In my opinion red quinoa is the perfect grain. I have tried this grain in almost every conceivable way possible and have yet to find any fault with it. From the flour in breads and soups to the whole grain in salads and desserts, use it and you too will fall in love with red quinoa.

Nutrient content: Red quinoa is slightly higher in fiber than white quinoa.

Rice, Long Grain, Brown

Rice is a cereal grass and belongs in the same family as oats, barley, rye, and wheat.

Brown rice has only the hull and a small amount of the bran removed, thus retaining more minerals and vitamins than highly processed polished rice. Brown rice is an excellent starch. It is rich in fiber, extremely low in sodium and fat, and cholesterol free. Brown rice includes thiamin, riboflavin, niacin, carbohydrates, phosphorous, magnesium, calcium, potassium, silicon, sodium, fat, iron, and protein.

A kernel of long-grain rice is about five times as long as it is wide. It keeps its beautiful, long, slender shape as it cooks. It cooks up very light and fluffy, not gluey, and each kernel is separate. Long-grain rice is well suited to pilafs, paellas, stuffings, rice salads, fried rice, and casseroles.

Brown rice should be stored in a cool, dry area. It can be stored in an airtight container in the refrigerator or freezer to prolong shelf life. Under these conditions, it can last from ten months to a year.

Nutrient content per 1 cup cooked long-grain brown rice:
216 calories   20 mg calcium   3 g dietary fiber   0 mg vitamin C
5 g protein   161 mg phosp.   0 RE vitamin A   3 mg niacin
2 g fat, 0 sat. fat   .8 mg iron   .19 mg thiamin   84 mg potassium
0 mg cholesterol   10 mg sodium   .05 mg riboflavin   45 g carbohydrate

Nutrient content per 1 cup cooked long-grain white rice:
267 calories   21 mg calcium   1 g dietary fiber   0 mg vitamin C
6 g protein   88 mg phosp.   0 RE vitamin A   3 mg niacin
1 g fat, 0 sat. fat   2.5 mg iron   .33 mg thiamin   72 mg potassium
0 mg cholesterol   2 mg sodium   .03 mg riboflavin   58 g carbohydrate

Rye

Rye, a common grain, has been around since the Middle Ages. Because of its heavy and coarse texture, primarily it was the poor who ate it. The wealthy, on the other hand, preferred a pure white loaf, regardless of its contents. Today rye is eaten by many people as well as animals.

This grain contains a substantial concentration of nutrients, including protein, iron, eleven B vitamins, vitamin E, various minerals, and trace elements. And don't forget lysine—rye has the highest percentage of this amino acid, topping all of the common grains. Because of all of these nutrients, rye has the reputation for building muscle and promoting energy and endurance.

Remember not to make bread with just rye flour. Rye is low in gluten so you will have to mix rye with high-gluten flour. This will help the bread to rise and will make it lighter in taste.

Rye is a splendid grain with a rich flavor and wonderful nutrients. I think that rye is so misunderstood. I remember eating it as a child and hating the strong flavor. It wasn't until many years later, after I left home, that I discovered how wonderful rye is. The bad taste that I had disliked for so long was not the rye but the caraway seed that most bakers add to the bread.

The other thing that I learned about rye bread is that most of the rye bread made in America contains very little rye. It does not have what it needs to make bread, so it must rely on white flour. So, next time you make bread, don't forget to add rye. You'll love it.

Nutrient content per 1/2 cup cooked rye:
98 calories   0 mg sodium   4 g protein   2 g dietary fiber
0 g fat   24 g carbohydrate

Spelt

This grain has been around since 5000 BC in what is now Iran. It has been grown and harvested in other countries, such as Germany, Italy, Switzerland, and other parts of Europe. Purity Foods reintroduced it into North America in 1987. Today spelt is becoming more popular with bakers, manufacturers, and consumers.

Spelt is unique in more ways than one. It has an incredibly strong hull, which protects the grain from pollutants and insects. This is an excellent characteristic, especially when it comes to storing this grain.

Also, spelt contains thirty percent more protein, more fat, and more amino acids than wheat. It also has a high mineral content and considerable amounts of B vitamins, magnesium, and fiber. Added to that wonderful list, it is water soluble, which makes it easier for your body to absorb the nutrients.

But what if you can't have wheat but would like to eat spelt? Spelt is actually considered an excellent alternative to wheat. Because this grain is unhybridized and contains low gluten, it may be just what you need. If you are wheat intolerant, we suggest that you consult with your doctor about using spelt as an alternative for wheat in your diet.

I am almost convinced that spelt is the Mother Grain, the "Staff of Life." For hundreds of years spelt was the grain used to make bread in almost every part of the world. It was not until the late 1800s, when wheat was introduced, that spelt took the back seat, not for lack of nutrition but rather lack of production. Wheat outproduced spelt by about eighty percent, so you can see it was an economic movement, not one based on nutrition.

Clearly, spelt is a fabulous grain, packed with nutrients and complex carbohydrates. It can be used in almost every recipe where wheat is mentioned—cereals, pastas, crackers, pancake mixes, cookies, and so on. With a little experimentation you can make spelt a large part of your diet.

THOSE WONDERFUL GRAINS II

Those of you who are whole wheat fanatics will want to try spelt. All that nutrition—and it bakes so much nicer than wheat. Plus, it is far lighter and easier to digest than wheat. You won't want to miss this opportunity to do something wonderful for your body. Go ahead and give spelt a try.

Nutrient content per 1/2 cup cooked spelt:
100 calories　　　0 mg sodium　　　4 g protein　　　3.5 g dietary fiber
1 g fat　　　　　26 g carbohydrate

Teff

Just like Popeye, this tiny grain is small yet powerful. Unbelievably, it takes one hundred fifty grains of teff to equal just one grain of wheat. And that's not all; teff surpasses wheat in nutritional content. Impossible, you say? Well, read on, my friend.

Teff originated in Ethiopia and is said to date as far back as 4,000 to 1000 BC. Teff seeds were found in bricks used for the Egyptian pyramids back in 3359 BC. This grain has quite a history. Ethiopians used it for a staple bread called injera. The batter was fermented for days and then cooked in large round flats. Because of its high iron content, Ethiopians have a low anemic ratio.

Not only is teff high in iron, it is also high in protein, carbohydrates, fiber, calcium, phosphorous, copper, aluminum, barium, and thiamin.

Teff can be used in many ways. It may be substituted for seeds, nuts, and other small grains. It can also be used to thicken soups, stews, gravies, and puddings. Teff tastes great in veggie burgers and can be used for stir-fry dishes and casseroles. There really is a lot you can do with teff. Besides enjoying teff's versatility, you can rest assured that you are getting a mighty helping of nutrients.

The one thing that I enjoy about this grain is its small size. It cooks up fast, but I prefer to use it with other grains. The flour is amazing. It adds a lot to baked goods in flavor and nutrition. It passes off well as a substitute for poppy seeds without contributing to the danger of failing a urine sample.

It makes a great breakfast cereal. Add it to oatmeal and other breakfast cereals. I also like to use it in my rice dishes. It sort of hides behind whatever you cook it with. It is perfect thrown in whole into pancakes and waffles, and I love to use it in pizza doughs—it adds a crispness that I thoroughly enjoy. Don't be afraid to use the smallest grain in the world to get some big results in the foods you prepare.

Nutrient content per 2-oz. serving of teff:
200 calories   10 mg sodium   7 g protein   250 mg potassium
1 g fat   41 g carbohydrate

Triticale

With a name like triticale, you might think that this grain is centuries old. Despite popular belief, however, triticale has actually only been around for a century. In fact, this cereal is a man-made progeny of wheat and rye and, as its inventor hoped, it inherited the best of both parents.

The journey that led to the discovery of triticale began in Scotland around 1875. A botanist named Stephen Wilson decided to follow a hunch and crossbreed the two grains, wheat and rye. The hybrid was found to be cute in appearance but bore no fruit. He tried several more times but felt frustrated after finding that all the results were either sterile or unpredictable in size and shape.

He consequently moved on to his next project, leaving others to figure out this impossible puzzle. It wasn't until the late 1930s that a man named Pierre Givaudon found a solution to this plant that lacked fertility. He suggested that they coat the plant with a corcous derivative called colchicines. This solved the problem, and soon triticale was sprouting all on its own.

Today many are unaware of this delicious grain that has twice the protein as rye and more amino acids than both wheat and rye. It was once said that triticale would end world hunger. Instead, it has become a no-name and will continue to be so until more become comfortable with its existence. With our new knowledge, triticale's future is up to you and me!

Nutrient content per 1 cup triticale flour:
439 calories   46 mg calcium   19 g dietary fiber   0 mg vitamin C
17 g protein   417 mg phosp.   0 RE vitamin A   3.7 mg niacin
2 g fat, 0 sat. fat 3.4 mg iron   .49 mg thiamin   605 mg potassium
0 mg cholesterol   3 mg sodium   .17 mg riboflavin   95 g carbohydrate

Nutrient content per 1/2 cup cooked triticale:
129 calories   .4 g fat   4 g dietary fiber   5 g protein
1.5 mg sodium   0 mg cholesterol   27 g carbohydrate

Wheat

It is unknown when this grain originated, but it is thought to have been 10,000 to 15,000 years BC. Considered by most Americans as the "Staff of Life," wheat is grown in many areas throughout the world.

Wheat contains thirteen B vitamins, vitamin E, protein, essential fatty acids, and important trace minerals. It also contains high amounts of gluten, the protein that provides the elasticity necessary for excellent bread making.

There are four major types of wheat available today: hard red, hard white, soft, and durum.

Hard red wheat is high in protein and is good for making breads. Hard white wheat, also high in iron, is more easily digestible than hard red wheat and makes a very light loaf of bread.

Soft wheat, low in protein and gluten, is used in making biscuits, pastries, cookies, and pancakes.

Durum wheat, the hardest wheat, is high in gluten and protein. It is used for pastas and noodles, as its hard starch granules hold pasta together in boiling water.

Nutrient content per 1 cup cooked wheat:
84 calories
4 g protein
<1 g fat, 0 sat. fat
0 mg cholesterol
9 mg calcium
78 mg phosp.
.9 mg iron
1 mg sodium
3 g dietary fiber
0 RE vitamin A
.12 mg thiamin
.03 mg riboflavin
0 mg vitamin C
1.5 mg niacin
99 mg potassium
20 g carbohydrate

Grains Cooking Chart

Grain	Ratio	Stovetop	Pressure*
Amaranth	1:3	8 min.	4 min.
Barley, Flakes	1:3	10 min.	6 min.
Barley, Pearled	1:3	25 min.	12 min.
Barley, Whole	1:3	12 min.	35 min.
Buckwheat, Hulled	1:3	22 min.	6 min.
Farro	1:2	45 min.	12 min.
Kamut®	1:3	60 min.	30 min.
Kamut®, Cracked	1:2	12 min.	6 min.
Kamut®, Flakes	1:2	12 min.	4 min.
Kasha, Roasted	1:3	12 min.	6 min.
Millet	1:2	16 min.	6 min.
Oat Groats	1:2	20 min.	6 min.
Oats, Rolled	1:3	20 min.	5 min.
Oats, Quick	1:3	8 min.	NR
Oats, Steel Cut	1:2	12 min.	4 min.
Quinoa, Black	1:2	18 min.	6 min.
Quinoa, Red	1:2	18 min.	6 min.
Quinoa, White	1:2	18 min.	5 min.
Rice, Brown	1:2	45 min.	14 min.
Rice, White	1:2	25 min.	6 min.
Rye, Berries	1:2	32 min.	15 min.
Rye, Flakes	1:3	30 min.	6 min.
Six-Grain	1:2	15 min.	NR
Spelt	1:3	60 min.	30 min.
Teff, Berries	1:4	6 min.	NR
Wheat, Berries	1:3	60 min.	30 min.
Wheat, Bulgur	1:2	6 min.	3 min.
Wheat, Cracked	1:2	12 min.	6 min.

*Most grains do well in the pressure cooker. Natural release method is recommended, meaning after suggested cooking time, turn off heat and let the pressure come down naturally. Those grains for which pressure cooking is not recommended are indicated "NR" (Not Recommended).

Those Wonderful Grains!

Grain	Gluten-Free	Fiber (per 1/2 cup)
Amaranth	Yes	2 g
Barley, Flakes	No	6 g
Barley, Pearled	No	3 g
Barley, Whole	No	5 g
Buckwheat, Hulled	Yes	3 g
Farro	No	8 g
Kamut®	No	6 g
Kamut®, Cracked	No	5 g
Kamut®, Flakes	No	5 g
Kasha, Roasted	Yes	4 g
Millet	Yes	2 g
Oat Groats	Yes	4 g
Oats, Rolled	Yes	3 g
Oats, Quick	Yes	2 g
Oats, Steel Cut	Yes	3 g
Quinoa, Black	Yes	3 g
Quinoa, Red	Yes	4 g
Quinoa, White	Yes	3 g
Rice, Brown	Yes	4 g
Rice, White	Yes	1 g
Rye, Berries	No/Low	6 g
Rye, Flakes	No/Low	4 g
Six-Grain	No	5 g
Spelt	No	3.5 g
Teff, Berries	Yes	15 g
Wheat, Berries	No	7 g
Wheat, Bulgur	No	9 g
Wheat, Cracked	No	5 g

Grains Cooking Chart

Grain	Salad	Soup	Yeasted Breads	Pancakes/ Pastries
Amaranth	Yes	Yes	Yes *	Yes*
Amaranth, Popped	Yes	Yes	Yes	Yes
Barley	Yes	Yes	Yes *	Yes*
Buckwheat	No	No	Yes *	Yes*
Bulgur Wheat	Yes	Yes	Yes	No
Corn, Field	No	No	Yes *	No
Farro	Yes	Yes	Yes *	Yes*
Kamut®	Yes	Yes	Yes *	Yes*
Kasha	Yes	Yes	Yes *	Yes*
Kasha, Roasted	Yes	Yes	Yes	No
Millet	Yes	Yes	Yes *	Yes*
Popcorn	No	No	Yes *	Yes
Oats	Yes	Yes	Yes *	Yes*
Quinoa, Black	Yes	Yes	Yes *	No
Quinoa, Red	Yes	Yes	Yes *	Yes*
Quinoa, White	Yes	Yes	Yes *	Yes
Rice, Brown	Yes	Yes	Yes *	Yes*
Rice, White	Yes	Yes	Yes *	Yes*
Rye	Yes	Yes	Yes *	Yes*
Spelt	Yes	Yes	Yes *	Yes*
Teff	No	Yes	Yes *	Yes*
Triticale	Yes	Yes	Yes *	Yes*
Wheat, Durum	No	No	Yes *	Yes
Wheat, Red	Yes	Yes	Yes *	Yes
Wheat, Soft	Yes	Yes	Yes *	Yes*
Wheat, White	Yes	Yes	Yes *	Yes*

*Flour made from this grain may also be used for this purpose.

Those Wonderful Grains!

Grain	Cookies/ Treats	Meat Substitutes	Non-Yeasted Breads/Cakes
Amaranth	Yes*	No	Yes*
Amaranth, Popped	Yes	No	Yes
Barley	Yes*	Yes	Yes*
Buckwheat	No	No	Yes
Bulgur Wheat	No	Yes	Yes
Corn, Field	No	No	No*
Farro	Yes*	Yes	Yes*
Kamut®	Yes*	Yes	Yes*
Kasha	No*	No	Yes*
Kasha, Roasted	No	Yes	Yes
Millet	Yes*	Yes*	Yes*
Popcorn	No	No	Yes
Oats	Yes*	Yes*	Yes*
Quinoa, Black	No	Yes	Yes
Quinoa, Red	Yes*	Yes*	Yes*
Quinoa, White	No	Yes	Yes*
Rice, Brown	Yes*	No	Yes*
Rice, White	Yes	No	No
Rye	Yes*	No	Yes*
Spelt	Yes*	Yes	Yes*
Teff	Yes*	No	Yes*
Triticale	Yes	No	Yes
Wheat, Durum	Yes	No	Yes
Wheat, Red	Yes	Yes	Yes
Wheat, Soft	Yes*	Yes	Yes*
Wheat, White	Yes	Yes	Yes*

Notes

Bread

Breads, the One-Third Rule

Breads are great way to add nutrition to your diet. I love to use grains in bread making. It has changed the way I make bread and increased the flavor and nutrition in my baking. There is a simple formula that, if followed, will add flair and excitement to bread making.

The formula is called the one-third rule: Just add any grain to your bread recipe as long as you do not exceed more than one-third of your total flour. For example, if your recipe calls for nine cups of flour, you can use up to three cups of any grain you want, in any form you desire. The grain can be flour, cracked, cooked, or whole. The other six cups of flour must be some form of wheat—red wheat, white wheat or white flour, and/or spelt.

If you will follow this simple formula, you will have great success in bread making. You can add any grain in any variety you desire, and you can mix the grains to add flavor and nutrition to your diet. If you like texture to your breads, you can add the grains cooked or raw. Some of the larger grains need to be cooked before using. Some can be cracked and cooked or just cracked. If you do not like the texture, just grind the grains into flour and combine the flours to create wonderful breads. Use a variety of different grains. Don't be tied down to just one type. I have used every grain in bread and love each one for different reasons.

If you are not sure about the amount of flour to use, it is simple: 1 cup of liquid in a recipe equals about three cups of flour.

The Formula:
1/3 grain + 2/3 wheat type flour = multi-grain breads

Super Grain Bread

Oh my! This is a great bread, packed with flavor. Try this one out for toast.

6 c. water
2/3 c. oil
1 c. honey
3 c. Super Grain Mix, ground
1 Tbsp. salt
2 Tbsp. dough enhancer
2 Tbsp. gluten
12–16 c. hard white wheat flour
3 Tbsp. Saf-Instant® or other instant yeast
1 c. high gluten bread flour (optional)

Place ingredients in Bosch bowl with yeast on top, holding back half of the flour. Gradually add in flour until dough pulls away from sides of bowl. Mix for 6 minutes. Shape into loaves. Preheat oven to 400 degrees. Place loaves in oven and immediately drop temperature to 325 degrees. Bake 25–30 minutes or until internal temperature reaches 180 degrees.

Yield: 6 loaves
Prep. Time: 10 min.
Cooking Time: 25–30 min.

Super Grain Mix:

1-1/2 c. whole buckwheat
1 c. sorghum
1 c. amaranth
1 c. black quinoa

Chef Brad tip

Gluten and dough enhancer are great to use when adding extra grains to breads.

Maple Quinoa Oat Bran Bread

Maple syrup makes a great sweetener and gives the bread a subtle flavor that I really enjoy.

1 c. pure maple syrup
5 c. hot milk (110 degrees)
1/2 c. canola oil
1 Tbsp. salt
1 c. oat bran
2 c. rolled oats

1 c. red quinoa, steamed
1 c. whole wheat flour
5 c. high gluten bread flour
1/4 c. Saf-Instant® or other instant yeast

Add all ingredients to Bosch bowl, placing flour in last with yeast on top of flour. Turn on Bosch bowl and add:

4–6 c. high gluten bread flour

Keep adding flour until dough pulls away from sides of bowl. Knead for 6 minutes, giving time for gluten to form. Remove from bowl and divide into freestanding loaves or loaves in pans. Let rise until double in size and bake in preheated 400-degree oven for 5 minutes, then drop the temperature to 325 degrees and bake for 25–30 minutes or until bread is done.

Yield: 5 loaves
Prep. Time: 10–15 min.
Cooking Time: 30–35 min.

Chef Brad tip

> Don't be afraid to use a little high gluten bread flour. It can really give the bread a little lift like nothing else can.

Hazelnut Multi-Grain Crackers

Try these with the Red Quinoa Onion Dip recipe on page 111. Light and tasty! You will not be able to eat just one.

1 c. (about 4-1/2 oz.) hazelnuts, toasted and skinned
1 c. blend of sorghum and buckwheat flour, freshly ground
1/3 c. Romano Parmesan cheese
1/2 tsp. salt
1-1/2 tsp. sugar
5 Tbsp. cold butter, cut into pieces
1 large egg, beaten
3 Tbsp. heavy cream

In blender, blend nuts to butter. With Bosch whips, blend flour, cheese, salt, and sugar. Add butter and mix until resembles coarse meal. With dough hook, stir in nut butter, and egg. Cream until dough is smooth. Divide dough in half and form logs. Freeze until logs are firm, about 1 hour. Preheat oven to 400 degrees. Cut logs in 1/3-inch slices and bake on parchment until just golden brown. You may have to turn crackers over for a couple minutes to complete baking. Crackers will crisp as they cool. Sprinkle with salt while still warm.

Prep. Time: 70 min. incl. freezing

For more information about ingredients and equipment, please check out Chef Brad's website, www.chefbrad.com, or email chef@chefbrad.com

Granola Bread

Sweet, tasty bread—great for toast or sandwiches.

3 c. unprepared granola (see recipe for Old-Fashioned Multi-Grain Granola, page 78)
1 c. sourdough starter
4 c. warm milk
1/3 c. canola oil
1/2 c. brown sugar
1 Tbsp. salt
3 eggs, beaten
1 Tbsp. vanilla extract
3 c. high gluten bread flour
6 c. hard white wheat flour, freshly ground, or spelt flour
3 Tbsp. Saf-Instant® or other instant yeast

Heat milk. Add warm milk, sourdough starter, oil, sugar, salt, vanilla, eggs, granola, and high gluten bread flour to Bosch bowl. Place yeast on top of flour and start Bosch. Start adding whole wheat or spelt flour to bowl. Continue adding until dough pulls away from sides of bowl. Knead for 6 minutes then remove dough from bowl and form into loaves. If you are making free-standing loaves, place on parchment paper and cut slits in top of loaf. Let rise until double. If using loaf pans, place bread in coated or sprayed pans and let rise until double, about 25–30 minutes. Bake in preheated 400-degree oven for 5 minutes, dropping temperature to 325 degrees for remainder of cooking time.

Yield: 4 loaves
Prep. Time: 15 min.
Cooking Time: 30 min.

Ethiopian Injera (Quick Method)

Injera is meant to be an eating surface and a flavor sponge as well as a wrapper for other foods. It is common to eat it with fingers, tearing off an edge of injera and then using it to pick up a mouthful of food. The flavors soak into the bread beautifully.

2 c. teff flour
3 c. hot water (110 degrees)
1/2 c. sourdough starter
2 tsp. Saf-Instant® or other instant yeast

Place teff flour into a bowl and add water, sourdough starter, and yeast. Mix well and cover with plastic wrap. Let set out overnight. To bake, heat nonstick pan and when pan is hot, stir batter (it should be thin). Ladle about 1/2 cup at a time onto hot pan in a drizzle, starting from outside of bowl and working to the center. Lift pan and spread batter evenly. Place lid on pan and bake 2 minutes or until bread starts to curl on edges. Place cooked bread in towel to keep warm and continue process.

Yield: 6–10
Prep. Time: 8 min.
Cooking Time: 2 min. each

Multi-Grain Beehive Bread

A little bit more work than the average bread but the end result is great. A perfect bread for that rainy afternoon. Read a good book while it is growing and baking and then be prepared for a treat.

  1/2 c. hot water (110 degrees)   2 tsp. Saf-Instant® or other
  2-3/4 c. plus 2 Tbsp. cool   instant yeast
   water (75 degrees)   2-1/2 c. sourdough starter

Combine yeast and hot water and stir to dissolve yeast. Let stand for 3 minutes. Add cool water and sourdough starter to yeast mixture and mix.

  1/2 c. black sesame seeds   1/2 c. amaranth, popped*
   (1/4 c. for bread mixture   1/2 c. millet seed
   and 1/4 c. for top of bread)   2/3 c. cornmeal
  1/2 c. teff   2-1/2 Tbsp. kosher salt

Add to sourdough mixture.

  8 c. blended flour mixture
   (4 c. durum flour and
   4 c. high gluten bread flour)

Add in flour until dough pulls away from sides of bowl. Mix for 6 minutes. Place in lightly oiled bowl. Refrigerate dough for at least 8 hours to let flavors develop and dough relax. Take from refrigerator and allow to warm up and rise slowly, about 1 hour. Divide dough into 4 parts. On lightly floured surface, gently flatten one piece of dough into rectangle then shape into cylinder by rolling it tightly from left to right. Seal seam well. Place both hands over center out to ends to elongate until you have a rope about 20 inches long. Roll rope lightly in flour and shape into coil.

Sprinkle cornmeal on parchment-lined paddle. Place seam side down. Lightly spray water into grooves of each coil and pour black sesame seeds into same grooves. Cover with oiled plastic wrap. Let rise for 1 hour or until doubled.

About 30 minutes before baking, preheat pizza stone and oven to 425 degrees. Place empty water pan directly below stone. Gently slide bread onto stone. Pour 1 cup of very hot water into water pan and immediately shut oven door. After 1 minute quickly mist loaves 6–8 times then quickly shut oven door. Mist again 1 minute later. Bake 20 minutes then reduce to 375 degrees and bake for 15 minutes until loaves are golden yellow and sound slightly hollow when tapped.

Yield: 2 loaves
Prep. Time: 2 hr.
Cooking Time: 35 min.

*For instructions on popping amaranth, see page 12.

Chef Brad tip
> Cooking time varies according to both the size of the loaves and variations in ovens.

Toasted Quinoa Cranberry Buttermilk Bread

Buttermilk and quinoa—what a wonderful combination! This recipe really is special, baked a little longer to assure a wonderful crust and a tender inside.

1 c. black quinoa toasted	2 tsp. dough enhancer
4 c. buttermilk	1/2 c. dried cranberries
3 Tbsp. lemon juice	8 c. whole wheat flour
3 eggs, slightly beaten	3 Tbsp. Saf-Instant®
1/3 c. honey	or other instant yeast
1/3 c. oil	High gluten bread flour
1 Tbsp. salt	

Toast black quinoa in skillet. Combine quinoa, buttermilk, lemon juice, eggs, honey, oil, salt, dough enhancer, and cranberries to Bosch bowl. Add whole wheat flour, placing yeast on top of flour. Turn on Bosch and add high gluten bread flour until dough pulls away from sides of bowl. Mix for 6 minutes. Remove from bowl and divide in 4 equal parts. Shape into round loaves and let rise until double. Bake for 5 minutes on preheated pizza stone at 400 degrees. Reduce heat and bake for another 20–25 minutes or until internal temperature reaches 210 degrees.

Yield: 4 loaves
Prep. Time: 10–15 min.
Cooking Time: 25–30 min.

Chef Brad tip

> A great marriage is like great bread; it blesses all who partake of it.

Apple, Teff, & Triticale Bread

You won't miss the white flour in this recipe. Try the variations and enjoy.

2-1/2 c. triticale flakes, ground	3 c. sugar
1 c. teff flour	2 tsp. baking soda
1 tsp. salt	4 eggs
2 tsp. cinnamon	3/4 c. oil
2 tsp. nutmeg	2/3 c. liquid
	2 c. applesauce

Mix wet and dry ingredients separately. Combine. Stir until moist and bake at 350 degrees for 20–25 minutes.

Variations:

Zucchini Bread:
Substitute 2/3 c. buttermilk for the 2/3 c. liquid; 2 c. grated zucchini for the 2 c. applesauce.

Fruit Bread:
Substitute 2 c. fructose for the 3 c. sugar.
Substitute 2/3 c. buttermilk for the 2/3 c. liquid.
Substitute 2 c. frozen berries for the 2 c. applesauce.
Add 1 tsp. Rumford baking powder.
Add 1 c. mangoes, pureed.

Yield: 1 loaf
Prep. Time: 5–10 min.
Cooking Time: 20–25 min.

Chef Brad tip

The secret to successful yeastless breads is to make sure you don't overmix.

Spelt Potato Nut Bread

French-style bread with a wonderful flavor and texture. I add just a little spelt white flour to lighten the loaves a little.

2 large potatoes, chopped
1 c. water

Pressure cook for 5 minutes on high, natural release. Place potatoes and water in Bosch blender and puree. Pour into bowl and add following ingredients:

2 c. hot water (110 degrees)	3 c. spelt flour, freshly ground
1 Tbsp. salt	2 Tbsp. Saf-Instant® or other instant yeast
2 Tbsp. sugar	White spelt flour
1 c. hemp nut, toasted	

Mix all ingredients in Bosch bowl, holding back white spelt flour with yeast on top. Mix, adding in white spelt flour as needed until dough cleans sides of bowl. Knead for 6 minutes. Roll into 2 french loaves. Let rise until double, about 30 minutes. Preheat oven to 400 degrees. Place loaves in oven for 5 minutes, then drop temperature to 325 degrees and bake approximately 40 minutess longer or until the inner temperature reaches 210 degrees. Spritz with water at 5-minute intervals.

Yield: 2 french loaves or 1 freestanding loaf
Prep. Time: 50 min. incl. rising
Cooking Time: 45–50 min.

Amaranth Olive Bread

The perfect combination—olives and grains.

4 c. hot water (110 degrees)
1 c. sourdough starter
3 Tbsp. olive oil
1 Tbsp. salt
1/2 c. kalamata olives, chopped
1/2 c. roasted red peppers, chopped
1/4 c. sugar
1/2 c. feta cheese
1 c. whole amaranth
2 c. cooked steel cut oats
9 c. flour, high gluten bread flour, or whole wheat flour
3 Tbsp. Saf-Instant® or other instant yeast

Place hot water in Bosch bowl. Add all remaining ingredients and half the flour, placing yeast on top. Turn on Bosch bowl and add remaining flour until dough pulls away from sides of bowl. Knead for 6 minutes. Remove from Bosch bowl and divide into 4 loaves. Form into round loaves and place on cornmeal-covered parchment paper on cookie sheets. Bake in 400-degree preheated oven for 5 minutes and drop the heat to 325 degrees for remaining time.

Yield: 4 loaves
Prep. Time: 15 min.
Cooking Time: 25 min. rising, 25–30 min. cooking

Chef Brad tip

Bread is done on the inside when it is 180 degrees. For a thicker, crustier bread, go to 210 degrees internal temperature.

Red Pepper Farro Bread

I make this bread into freestanding loaves. I also cook it a little longer to develop a nice crust.

- 2 c. farro, cooked
- 2 c. farro flour
- 4 c. hot water (110 degrees)
- 1 c. sourdough starter
- 1/4 c. olive oil
- 1/4 c. sugar
- 1 Tbsp. salt
- 1 c. feta cheese
- 1/2 c. roasted red peppers, (canned) chopped
- 9 c. high gluten bread flour (approx.)
- 3 Tbsp. Saf-Instant® or other instant yeast

Place cooked farro and farro flour in Bosch bowl with water, sourdough starter, olive oil, sugar, salt, cheese, roasted peppers, and 5 cups of high gluten bread flour. Place yeast on top of flour and turn on mixer. Add enough remaining flour until dough pulls away from the sides of bowl. Mix for 6 minutes. Remove from bowl and divide into loaves. Let rise until double in size. Bake in 400-degree oven for 5 minutes, dropping temperature to 325 degrees for the remaining time. Internal temperature should be 210 degrees.

Yield: 3 loaves
Prep. Time: 10 min.
Cooking Time: 35 min.

Chef Brad tip

Farro cooks like brown rice, about 12 minutes in the pressure cooker or 45 minutes on the stovetop.

Brown Rice Spanish Bread

Baking on a hot pizza stone is perfect for this recipe.

3 c. hot water (110 degrees)
1/4 c. olive oil
1 Tbsp. salt
1 c. brown rice, steamed or cooked
6 c. whole wheat, freshly ground, or high gluten bread flour
1-1/2 Tbsp. Saf-Instant® or other instant yeast

Place water, oil, salt, rice, and 4 cups of the flour in Bosch mixer. Place yeast on top of flour. Turn on Bosch and add remaining flour, as needed, until dough pulls away from sides of bowl. Mix for 5 minutes in Bosch. Remove from bowl and place in oiled bowl and cover. Let rise until double, about 30 minutes. After bread has risen to double, remove from bowl and divide into 2 pieces. Form loaves, cutting slits in top of bread. Place them on cookie sheet or cornmeal-covered parchment paper. Let rise until double. Place in 400-degree oven and bake until dark golden brown, about 20–30 minutes. It should sound really hollow when tapped on. Enjoy!

Yield: 2 loaves
Prep. Time: 12 min.
Cooking Time: 25–30 min. rising, 20–30 min. cooking

Chef Brad tip

A pizza stone holds the heat. This is wonderful for freestanding loaves.

THOSE WONDERFUL GRAINS II

Bolillos

A very South American bread. Wonderfully satisfying.

1 c. water
1 Tbsp. Saf-Instant® or other instant yeast
1/2 tsp. sugar
1 c. lukewarm milk
1 c. amaranth, popped*

6-1/2 c. high gluten bread flour
1 Tbsp. salt
1-1/2 tsp. Rumford baking powder
Vegetable oil for coating
2 Tbsp. butter, softened

To make sponge, combine in Bosch bowl water, yeast, and sugar. Mix until dissolved. Add milk, amaranth, and 1-1/2 cups of flour and mix until smooth. Set aside for 30 minutes. To sponge, add salt, baking powder, and enough of remaining flour that dough pulls away from sides of bowl. Knead for 6 minutes. Divide dough into 9 portions and roll each into a ball. Set aside to rest for 10 minutes. In small bowl, knead together soft butter and 1 tablespoon flour. Pull each dough ball into 6-inch log. With knife make shallow slit down center of each log and spread some of butter mixture inside. Enclose by briefly rolling on counter and then transfer face down to baking sheet. Let rise 30–45 minutes or until double in size. Put 1 cup water and 1 tablespoon of salt in spray bottle and mix. Spray rolls generously with salt water mixture. Bake 5 minutes at 425 degrees, then turn down temperature to 325 degrees and bake 10–20 minutes or until golden brown. Do not overbake.

Yield: 9
Prep. Time: 1 hr. 45 min. incl. rising
Cooking Time: 15–25 min.

*For instructions on popping amaranth, see page 12.

Multi-Grain Bread Sticks

Hot bread makes a meal, and these bread sticks are so easy—and what a taste! You better double the batch; they go really fast.

1 c. boiling water
1/4 c. quinoa
1/4 c. amaranth
1/4 c. teff
2 Tbsp. pizza seasoning

Place grain in boiling water and let set while preparing rest of recipe. In Bosch bowl combine the following:

1 c. sourdough starter
2 c. water
4 Tbsp. basil oil
2 Tbsp. salt
4 Tbsp. sugar
8 oz. feta cheese
1/2 c. kalamata olives, chopped
3 c. (to start) high gluten bread flour
4 Tbsp. Saf-Instant® or other instant yeast

Add soaked grains and seasonings to above mixture. Start Bosch mixing and add high gluten bread flour until dough cleans sides of the bowl. Mix for 6–8 minutes. Remove from bowl. Let proof or rise 30 minutes. Roll out flat. Brush with basil oil and sprinkle with freshly grated Romano Parmesan cheese. Cut into strips, twist, and place on parchment. Bake on preheated 500-degree pizza stone for 5–7 minutes.

Yield: 3 doz.
Prep. Time: 45–50 min. incl. rising
Cooking Time: 5–7 min.

Chef Brad tip

> Most pizza doughs make great bread sticks. Save the extra dough for the next day and bake them fresh.

Sweet Teff French Bread

Teff really gives this bread a wonderful look and taste.

8 c. high gluten bread flour
2 Tbsp. salt, preferably
Sea salt
3 c. water

1/2 c. teff
2 Tbsp. Saf-Instant® or
other instant yeast

Place water, teff, salt, 4-1/2 cups flour in Bosch bowl, with yeast on top, and mix. Add in additional flour until dough pulls away from sides of bowl. Knead for 6 minutes. Cover with either damp towel or plastic wrap or put bowl into a plastic bag. Leave dough out at room temperature to rise, about 1-1/2 hours. Dough will have doubled in size. Punch it down, form into a ball, return to the bowl, and allow it to rise again for 1 to 1-1/2 hours or until double. Punch it down again. Form into loaves and let rise until double.

When ready to bake, slash tops of loaves diagonally (3 slashes are usually sufficient) or, for round loaves, in tic-tac-toe or an asterisk pattern. Spray loaves with cold water and place on preheated 425-degree oven (375-degree convection oven). After 2 minutes quickly spray loaves again. Two minutes later spray again. Two minutes later, give another spray. You may want to rotate pans 180 degrees after final spray if oven is baking unevenly. About 10 minutes after last spray, look at loaves. If they appear to be golden brown and done, turn off oven and allow loaves to cook in a cooling oven for 10 more minutes. Total cooking time is 26–30 minutes for baguettes and up to 40 minutes for larger loaves. Remove the bread from oven and allow to cool for 20–45 minutes. Serve.

Yield: 3 french loaves
Prep. Time: 3 to 3-1/2 hrs. incl. rising
Cooking Time: 26–30 min.

Sourdough Kalamata French Bread

Don't be afraid to use those wonderful kalamata olives. They really add to the bread.

1-1/2 c. hot water (110 degrees)
1/4 c. powdered milk
1-1/2 Tbsp. shortening
2 tsp. salt
3 Tbsp. sugar
4–8 c. spelt white flour

1/2 c. kalamata olives, chopped
1 c. sourdough starter
1-1/2 Tbsp. Saf-Instant® or other instant yeast
Egg Wash (topping)

Place all ingredients, except half the flour, in Bosch bowl with yeast on top. Turn on Bosch and add spelt flour until it cleans sides of bowl. Knead for 6 minutes. Form into loaves. Let rise until double. Brush with Egg Wash and bake at 350 degrees for 30–35 minutes or until bread thermometer reaches 180 degrees.

Yield: 2 loaves
Prep. Time: 10 min.
Cooking Time: 30–35 min.

Egg Wash:
1 egg
2 Tbsp. water

Blend together well.

Buckwheat Amaranth Rolls

Freshly ground buckwheat really adds a great look to bread—not to mention a fabulous taste.

2 c. milk
1/2 c. butter or oil
1/2 c. sugar
2 tsp. salt
2 eggs

8–10 c. high gluten bread flour
2 Tbsp. Saf-Instant® or other instant yeast
1 c. amaranth, popped*
1/4 c. buckwheat, ground

Scald milk or use powdered milk mixed according to directions. Add butter, sugar, amarath, buckwheat, salt, and 2 cups of high-gluten flour. Mix until smooth. Beat in egg and yeast. Add flour until dough cleans bowl. Shape into rolls and place in greased pan, with rolls barely touching each other. Let rise until double in bulk. Bake at 350 degrees for 20–25 minutes.

Yield: 2 doz.
Prep. Time: 15 min.
Cooking Time: 20–25 min.

*For instructions on popping amaranth, see page 12.

Mango Amaranth Rolls

Mangoes add a wonderful flavor to anything. I love the flavor and texture of these rolls. Remember to keep the dough sticky for lighter rolls.

1 c. boiling water
1 c. cracked wheat

Cover cracked wheat with water and let set. In Bosch bowl combine:

1-1/2 c. sourdough starter
3 c. hot water (110 degrees)
1/2 c. honey
1/3 c. canola oil
2 tsp. dough enhancer

1 Tbsp. salt
3/4 c. mangoes, pureed
1 c. amaranth, popped*
2 Tbsp. Saf-Instant® or other instant yeast

Combine cracked wheat to above mixture. Add high gluten bread flour until dough pulls away from sides. Knead for 6 minutes. Roll out into rolls and let rise until double in size. Cook at 400 degrees for 5 minutes, then turn heat down to 325 degrees for 15–20 minutes.

Yield: 3 doz.
Prep. Time: 10–15 min.
Cooking Time: 20–25 min.

*For instructions on popping amaranth, see page 12.

Amaranth Oat Dinner Rolls

The secret to great dinner rolls is to make the dough sticky. This roll is light and the grains add a rustic quality that makes it the perfect companion for soups.

- 3 c. hot milk (110 degrees)
- 2 eggs
- 1/2 c. butter (1 stick.), melted
- 1/2 c. sugar
- 1 Tbsp. salt
- 1 c. amaranth (popped,* optional)
- 2 tsp. dough enhancer
- 2 c. steel cut oats
- 6 c. high gluten bread flour
- 2 Tbsp. Saf-Instant® or other instant yeast

Heat milk and stick of butter to 110 degrees. Place in Bosch bowl and add sugar, salt, dough enhancer, amaranth, and oats. Place 4 cups of flour on top of ingredients with yeast on top of flour. Turn on Bosch and start mixing. Add enough remaining flour until dough starts to pull away from side of bowl. Remember, you need to leave dough a little sticky for dinner rolls. When desired stickiness is obtained, knead dough for 6 minutes. Remove from pan and form into rolls. Let rise to double in size. Bake in preheated 350-degree oven for 15–20 minutes.

Yield: 4 doz.
Prep. Time: 15 min.
Cooking Time: 25–30 min. rising, 15-20 min. cooking

*For instructions on popping amaranth, see page 12.

Chef Brad tip

Create a memory; take a friend some hot rolls.

Buckwheat Feta Pizza Dough

Don't be afraid of the beer. If you are, try using a non-alcoholic brand. Beer has been used for hundreds of years in making great breads.

1 bottle warm beer	1/4 c. feta cheese
1 c. hot water (110 degrees)	2 c. whole buckwheat flour, freshly ground
2 Tbsp. oil	
4 Tbsp. sugar	2 c. Tbsp. Saf-Instant® or or other instant yeast
2 tsp. salt	
1 Tbsp. dried dill weed	4 c. high gluten bread flour

In Bosch bowl place beer, water, sugar, salt, oil, dill weed, and feta cheese. Add buckwheat flour to mixture with yeast on top of flour. Turn on Bosch and start adding high gluten bread flour until dough pulls away from sides of bowl. Knead for 6 minutes. Remove from bowl and place in slightly oiled bowl and cover. Let rise until double. After dough has risen to double, remove from bowl and divide into 2 or 3 pieces. Roll out on cornmeal, semolina, or flour. Add desired toppings and bake on 500-degree pizza stone.

Yield: 3 thin or 2 thick crust pizzas
Prep. Time: 30–40 min. incl. rising
Cooking Time: 5–8 min.

Tender Pizza Dough

Tender and light. You will love it.

- 1-1/2 c. tofu drink mix
- 1 c. sourdough starter
- 2 Tbsp. base vegetable stock
- 1/4 c. olive oil
- 1/4 c. honey
- 1/3 c. rye berries
- 1/3 c. barley
- 2–3 c. high gluten bread flour
- 3 large Tbsp. Saf-Instant® or other instant yeast

Grind rye and barley. Place tofu milk, sourdough starter, vegetable base, oil, honey, and freshly ground flours in mixer bowl with yeast on top of flour. Turn on Bosch and add high gluten bread flour until dough pulls away from sides of bowl. Knead for 6 minutes and let set for about 20 minutes. Roll out and bake on preheated 500-degree pizza stone for 5–8 minutes.

Yield: 2 thin or 1 thick crust pizza
Prep. Time: 30 min.
Cooking Time: 5–8 min.

Crispy Super Grain Pizza Dough

Our thanks to Sue Locke for helping us with this recipe.

3 c. hot water (110 degrees)
1 tsp. brown sugar
2 tsp. sea salt
1 Tbsp. dough enhancer
1/2 c. Super Grain Mix, ground between fine and medium (see page 43)
2 large eggs, beaten
1 c. hard white wheat flour ground between fine and medium
2 Tbsp. Saf-Instant® or other instant yeast
3 c. high gluten bread flour

In Bosch bowl combine ingredients, except high gluten bread flour, with yeast on top. Begin mixing, adding white flour until dough cleans sides of bowl. Knead for 6 minutes to develop gluten. Let rest 20–30 minutes. Bake directly on hot pizza stone covered with parchment paper at 500 degrees for 5–8 minutes.

Yield: 5 12-inch crusts
Prep. Time: 30 min.
Cooking Time: 5–8 min.

Chef Brad tip

When measuring grains, make them well-rounded cupsful.

For more information about ingredients and equipment, please check out Chef Brad's website, www.chefbrad.com, or email chef@chefbrad.com

Multi-Grain Black Bean Pizza Dough

Black beans add flavor and texture to dough. I love the look of this dough. It just goes to prove, healthful can taste wonderful.

- 1/2 c. black bean flour
- 1 c. sourdough starter
- 1 c. black quinoa, cooked
- 1 c. bulgur wheat, cooked
- 3 c. hot water (110 degrees)
- 1/4 c. olive oil
- 1/4 c. sugar
- 1 Tbsp. salt
- 1 Tbsp. dough enhancer
- 2 c. hard white wheat flour
- 1/4 c. Saf-Instant® or other instant yeast
- High gluten bread flour

Grind beans. Cook grains like you would cook white rice; they cook together very well. Add hot water, olive oil, sugar, salt, quinoa, bulgur wheat, sourdough starter, bean flour, dough enhancer, and wheat flour to Bosch bowl with yeast on top. Start Bosch, adding enough high gluten bread flour until dough pulls away from sides of bowl. Knead for 6 minutes to develop gluten. Remove from bowl and let rise until double. Roll out and form into pizzas. Top with favorite ingredients and bake on 500-degree preheated pizza stone for 5–8 minutes.

Yield: 3 thin or 2 thick crusts
Prep. Time: 30–40 min. incl. rising
Cooking Time: 5–8 min.

Spelt Sourdough Pizza

This is a high-protein pizza dough. Spelt is very high in protein.

2 c. water
1/4 c. tofu drink mix
2 Tbsp. olive oil
2 Tbsp. honey
2 Tbsp. Dough Easy

1 c. sourdough starter
1 heaping Tbsp. salt
5 c. whole spelt flour
4 Tbsp. Saf-Instant® or other instant yeast

Add all ingredients to Bosch bowl with yeast on top. Turn on Bosch and start mixing. Add in more whole spelt flour (approximately 3 cups) until dough pulls away from sides of bowl. Mix for 6 minutes. Let dough set for about 20 minutes. Divide dough into balls and roll out into pizzas (4 thin crust pizzas or 2 thick crust pizzas). Bake on preheated 500-degree pizza stone for 5–7 minutes.

Yield: 4 thin or 2 thick crust pizzas
Prep. Time: 30 min. incl. rising
Cooking Time: 5–7 min.

Chef Brad tip

Dough Easy helps the dough relax. Although all my doughs do not ask for it, I love to use it and recommend it highly.

Popped Amaranth Focaccia & Pizza Dough

Focaccia is fast and easy. It's always a crowd-pleaser and it always turns out.

1 c. hot water (110 degrees)
3 Tbsp. Saf-Instant® or other instant yeast

Let set for 3 minutes. Then add:

1 c. sourdough starter
3 Tbsp. sugar
2 c. pastry flour

Mix for 30 seconds. Let sponge for 10 minutes. Add:

2 c. amaranth, popped*
1 Tbsp. salt
2 Tbsp. olive oil

2 c. cool water (75 degrees)
High gluten bread flour

Gradually add high gluten bread flour until dough pulls away from sides of bowl. Mix for 6 minutes. Roll out and place on parchment-lined paddle. Let rise. Make finger wells in dough.

Olive oil
Rosemary

Brush with olive oil and sprinkle with rosemary. Bake on preheated 500-degree pizza stone for 7–10 minutes.

Yield: 2
Prep. Time: 40 min. incl. rising
Cooking Time: 7–10 min.

*For instructions on popping amaranth, see page 12.

Sourdough Sorghum & Buckwheat Pizza Dough

I adore buckwheat in breads. It adds so much to the appeal of the dough, not to mention its wonderful earthy flavor.

- 1 c. sourdough starter
- 2 c. hot water (110 degrees)
- 2 Tbsp. sugar
- 1 c. sorghum flour, freshly ground
- 1 c. buckwheat flour, freshly ground
- 3 Tbsp. Saf-Instant® or other instant yeast
- High gluten bread flour

Place above ingredients in Bosch bowl and let sponge for 20 minutes with lid on. Then add following ingredients, adding just enough high gluten bread flour until dough pulls away from sides of bowl:

- 1 Tbsp. salt
- 2 Tbsp. olive oil
- 4–6 c. high gluten bread flour

With dough hook, mix for 6 minutes. Remove dough from bowl and set in oiled bowl and cover until double in size.

For pizza, roll out dough on a semolina-covered board to desired thickness. Bake on 500-degree preheated pizza stone for 5–7 minutes.

For hard rolls, divide dough into small balls and place on baking sheet, letting rise to double. Bake at 350 degrees until dark brown, 20–25 minutes.

Yield: 4 thin crust pizzas or 2 doz. rolls
Prep. Time: 50 min. incl. rising
Cooking Time: 5–7 min. for pizza; 20–25 min. for rolls

Multi-Grain Focaccia

This bread is packed with nutrition and flavor.

1-1/2 c. hot water (110 degrees)
4 Tbsp. honey
1 Tbsp. salt
3 Tbsp. olive oil
1 c. sourdough starter
1 c. whole wheat flour
1/4 c. quinoa
1/4 c. millet
1/4 c. Kamut®
1/4 c. brown rice
3 Tbsp. Saf-Instant® or other instant yeast

Grind grains. Add all ingredients to Bosch bowl including freshly ground grains with yeast on top. Turn on Bosch and start mixing.

1 c. high gluten bread flour (approx.)
Olive oil
Rosemary

Add high gluten bread flour until dough pulls away from sides of bowl. Mix for 6 minutes. Divide dough and roll out. Place on parchment paper on paddle. Let rise for 30 minutes. Make finger wells in dough and fill with olive oil. Top with rosemary. Bake on preheated 500-degree pizza stone for 7–10 minutes.

Yield: 2–3
Prep. Time: 45 min. incl. rising
Cooking Time: 7–10 min.

Chef Brad tip

It is worth investing in a good pizza stone to assure great baked products. A good stone will actually improve the overall performance of your oven.

Spelt Teff Focaccia

Teff is that wonderful grain that does not need to be cooked or ground. I just love adding it to recipes. So easy—and I think it looks just great.

2 c. hot water (110 degrees)	1 Tbsp. dough enhancer
2 c. sourdough starter	1 c. teff
4 Tbsp. oil	5–8 c. spelt flour
4 Tbsp. sugar	4 Tbsp. Saf-Instant® or
1 Tbsp. salt	other instant yeast

Place water, sourdough starter, oil, sugar, salt, dough enhancer, and teff in Bosch bowl. Add part of the flour with yeast on top. Turn on Bosch and mix, adding flour until dough pulls away from sides of bowl. Knead for 6 minutes. Remove from bowl and divide into 3 equal parts. Roll out dough and let rise until about 2 inches thick. Make indents in dough using fingers. Brush liberal amount of olive oil on dough. Sprinkle with rosemary and bake on preheated 500-degree pizza stone for about 7 minutes. Remove from oven and sprinkle with kosher salt.

Yield: 3
Prep. Time: 40–45 min. incl. rising
Cooking Time: 7–10 min.

Chef Brad tip

> Teff is the smallest grain in the world and is considered one of the healthiest.

Old World Christmas Focaccia

Great for the holidays but why suffer all year without this great bread? Toothsome is the best way to describe this focaccia bread.

1 c. hot water (110 degrees)	1/4 c. sugar
3 Tbsp. sugar	1/2 c. bacon, crisp
2 Tbsp. olive oil	2 shallots
1 Tbsp. salt	1 c. fresh cranberries, chopped
3 c. high gluten bread flour	2 Tbsp. Saf-Instant® or other instant yeast
3 egg whites	
1 c. sourdough starter	

Place all ingredients in Bosch bowl and add flour until dough pulls away from side of bowl. Mix for 6 minutes. Place in oiled bowl, cover, and let rise until double. Punch down, divide dough into 2, and roll out. Place on parchment-lined paddle. Let rise.

Olive oil
Rosemary

Punch finger holes in dough. Brush with olive oil and sprinkle with rosemary. Bake on preheated 500-degree pizza stone for 5–7 minutes.

Yield: 2
Prep. Time: 25–30 min. incl. rising
Cooking Time: 5–7 min.

Breakfast Foods

For a Breakfast Truly Fit for Champions, Choose Grains

Breakfast is considered the most important meal of the day. It should be thought out and planned to include plenty of fiber, and grains add that necessary fiber to our diet. Children especially need to have a high-fiber breakfast to start the day. Pop Tarts and most cold cereals are devoid of nutrition and especially of fiber. The leading cold cereals have only about two grams of fiber per serving—not enough fiber to enjoy better health.

Grains are a wonderful way to start the day. They can be tasty, nutritious, and fun to eat. There are many other choices besides wheat and oatmeal for breakfast—not to downgrade wheat and oatmeal—both are wonderful. There are other grains, however, that work well, providing much needed nutrition and fiber.

All the grains can be ground into flour and used in pancakes and waffles. Most all the grains can be cooked and eaten as breakfast cereals, hot or cold. The cooked grains can be added to eggs and potato dishes, enhancing the flavor and textures. Chilled cooked grains can be placed in yogurt, smoothies, muffins, and almost any breakfast selection.

What a great way to start the day—fiber-rich breakfast foods using whole grains. I have found that when I start the day eating high fiber, I make better food choices all day long and I feel better.

BREAKFAST FOODS

Mango Banana Nut Bread

Double the batch. It will not last long and you will want to share with a neighbor.

6 bananas, mashed
1 c. mangoes, pureed
3/4 c. shortening
1-1/2 c. milk
2 Tbsp. white vinegar
1 Tbsp. baking soda
3 c. sugar
1 tsp. salt
4-1/2 c. soft white wheat flour
1/2 c. nuts, chopped
2 c. rice, quinoa, and millet (combination), cooked

Preheat oven to 350 degrees. In Bosch bowl cream together bananas, mangoes, shortening, and sugar. Add vinegar to milk in large container. Add baking soda. It will foam a lot. Mix with creamed mixture. Add flour, salt, grains, and nuts. Mix well. Bake in sprayed pans for 50 minutes or until toothpick comes out clean.

Yield: 4 loaves
Prep. Time: 10 min.
Cooking Time: 50 min.

Chef Brad tip

I have found that sharing my creations with neighbors adds zest to their lives and brings joy to me.

Cranberry Buckwheat Muffins

If you are going to make muffins, please add other flours besides white.

1-1/3 c. dried cranberries
3/4 c. sugar
3 Tbsp. fresh orange juice
1-1/4 c. high gluten bread flour
1 c. buckwheat flour, freshly ground
1-1/2 Tbsp. Rumford baking powder
1/2 tsp. baking soda
1 tsp. salt
2 eggs
8 Tbsp, unsalted butter, melted
1/2 c. buttermilk (approx.)

Combine cranberries with 1/2 cup of the sugar and orange juice in medium-sized bowl. Let stand for 30 minutes. Preheat oven to 375 degrees. Grease or spray 12-cup muffin tin. In Bosch, beat eggs with butter until smooth. Stir in cranberries with all their liquid. Add flours, remaining 1/4 cup sugar, baking powder, baking soda, and salt. Stir in enough buttermilk to make soft batter. Do not overbeat! Fill muffin cups about 3/4 full. Bake until firm and golden brown, about 15 minutes. Cool tin on rack for 10 minutes before unmolding muffins.

Yield: 1 doz.
Prep. Time: 35 min. incl. standing time
Cooking Time: 15 min.

Multi-Grain Mango Coffee Cake

You don't have to like coffee to enjoy this cake. Cocoa or tea will do.

1/2 c. red quinoa, steamed
2-1/2 c. Kamut®/farro flour
1 c. sugar
1-1/3 Tbsp. Rumford baking powder
3/4 tsp. cinnamon
1/4 tsp. nutmeg
1/3 tsp. salt
1 c. buttermilk
1/3 c. canola oil
2 eggs, well beaten
3/4 tsp. vanilla extract

Preheat oven to 350 degrees. Lightly oil 8 x 8-inch pan. For batter, combine first 7 ingredients in medium bowl. Make a well in center. Combine buttermilk, oil, eggs, and vanilla. Add all at once to flour mixture. Stir until dry ingredients are moistened and liquid is evenly distributed. Pour batter into pan.

Topping:

2 c. whole mangoes, peeled, seeded, and chopped
1/4 c. sugar
3/4 tsp. cinnamon
1/4 c. pecans, chopped

Spread mangoes over top of batter. Combine sugar and cinnamon. Spoon over mangoes. Sprinkle with pecans. Bake at 350 degrees for 40 minutes or until wooden pick inserted in center comes out clean.

Yield: 9–12 servings
Prep. Time: 10 min.
Cooking Time: 40 min.

Blueberry Syrup

Move aside maple syrup, I have found a new favorite.

- 4 c. water
- 2 c. sugar
- 1 c. lemon juice
- 1 c. fresh blueberries

Combine and cook until blueberries are soft and sugar is dissolved. Add:

- 1/3 c. Ultra Gel or other thickening agent (to desired thickness)

Store in refrigerator.

Old-Fashioned Multi-Grain Granola

Tasty and satisfying. You won't just want to eat it for breakfast.

- 4 c. rolled oats
- 2 c. rolled barley or wheat flakes
- 2 c. quinoa flakes
- 2 c. red quinoa, popped
- 2 c. millet, toasted
- 1 c. almonds, sliced
- 2 c. pumpkin seeds
- 2 c. sunflower seeds
- 1-1/2 c. pecans
- 1-1/2 c. cashews
- 2 c. unsweetened coconut
- 1/2 c. flax meal
- 1 c. dried cranberries or raisins

Mix all ingredients in large bowl. In saucepan, heat below mixture until dissolved:

- 1 c. canola oil
- 2-1/2 c. honey
- 1 Tbsp. vanilla extract
- 1/2 tsp. nutmeg
- 1 tsp. cinnamon
- 2 tsp. salt
- 2 tsp. maple flavoring

Breakfast Foods

Pour heated mixture over grain mixture. Stir until grain mixture is moist. Spray a large pan or cover with parchment paper. Pour mixture on pan and spread evenly. Do not overfill pan. Bake in preheated 350-degree oven for 10–15 minutes or until golden brown, stirring to bake evenly. Remove from pan and cool. Store in airtight container—if it lasts that long!

Variation:

Add raisins or cranberries during last 5 minutes of baking. To pop or toast grains, place them in hot sauté pan without oil or water. Stir frequently.

Yield: 6 dry qt.
Prep. Time: 25 min.
Cooking Time: 10–15 min.

Chef Brad tip

Be careful not to overbake; the granola should be golden brown in color.

Maple Glazed Fiber Rich Breakfast Bread

This is a wonderful bread to make. It's fast and easy. Fills the basic needs for breakfast. Nutrition and sweetening combine to make this wonderful bread.

2 c. hot milk (110 degrees)
1 c. sourdough starter
3 eggs
1/3 c. sugar
2 c. Super Fiber Blend (see page 81)
1 Tbsp. salt
1/2 c. butter (1 stick), softened
1 tsp. cinnamon
1/2 tsp. nutmeg
1 c. dried cranberries
1 c. nuts, chopped
6 c. high gluten bread flour
3 Tbsp. Saf-Instant® or other instant yeast

Preheat oven and pizza stone to 500 degrees. Place Super Fiber Blend in Bosch bowl with dough hook. Add milk, sourdough starter, eggs, sugar, salt, soft butter, cinnamon, nutmeg, cranberries, and nuts. Place half of the flour on top with yeast on top of flour. Turn on Bosch and continue adding flour until dough pulls away from sides of bowl. Knead for 6 minutes. Remove from bowl and divide into 3 or 4 equal parts. Roll into 1/2-inch thick circles. Place on parchment paper. Let rise for 15–20 minutes. After bread has risen, you can brush with butter or cut into stripes and twist. Return to parchment and bake on a pizza stone. If you do not cut into strips, bake like a pizza on stone. Both strips or bread bake in about 5–7 minutes. After baking, glaze with Maple Glaze.

Maple Glaze:

4 Tbsp. butter, melted
2 tsp. maple extract
4 c. powdered sugar
1/4 c. milk or heavy cream

Whisk together until well blended. Drizzle over bread or twist. Eat and enjoy.

Yield: 3–4 breakfast breads
Prep. Time: 30 min. incl. rising
Cooking Time: 7 min.

Zucchini Muffins

Every time I make these I wonder how can I forget how wonderful they are.

4 eggs
2-1/8 c. sugar
1-2/3 c. salad oil
1-1/4 tsp. vanilla extract
4-1/4 c. zucchini, shredded
1/2 c. flax meal
2-3/4 c. Kamut® flour

2 tsp. Rumford baking powder
1-1/4 tsp. salt
2 tsp. baking soda
1-1/3 Tbsp. cinnamon
1-1/3 c. nuts
1-1/3 c. raisins

In Bosch mixing bowl with whips, mix first 4 ingredients to a mayonnaise-like texture. Change attachment to dough hook and add remaining ingredients. Place in sprayed muffin tins and bake at 350 degrees for 20 minutes.

Yield: 2–3 doz.
Prep. Time: 10 min.
Cooking Time: 20 min.

Super Fiber Blend:

2 c. oatmeal
1 c. flax seed
1 c. oat bran
1/2 c. chia seed
1-1/2 c. amaranth, popped*

Use this blend to add extra fiber in recipes.

*For instructions on how to pop amaranth, see page 12.

Super Grain Pineapple Banana Loaf

Packed with nutrition and flavor.

2 c. sugar or fructose
4 eggs
1-1/2 c. milk
1/3 c. vegetable oil
1/2 tsp. salt
1-1/2 tsp. baking soda
1 tsp. vanilla extract

2 large bananas, mashed
1 can (20 oz.) crushed pineapple
1 c. nuts (hazelnuts), chopped
3-1/2 c. Super Grain Mix, freshly ground (see page 43)

Combine ingredients and place in coated pans. Bake at 350 degrees in preheated oven for 45 minutes or until knife comes out clean.

Yield: 2 large loaves
Prep. Time: 5–10 min.
Cooking Time: 45 min.

Chef Brad tip

> Don't be a fanatic about health. Simply use good sense and variety in the foods you prepare. You'll keep your friends longer.

Basic Pancakes

Basic but outstanding. The vanilla pudding really adds flavor and texture.

- 1/3 c. vanilla instant pudding powder
- 1/3 c. tofu drink mix
- 3 eggs
- 1/4 c. oil
- 1 tsp. salt
- 4 c. water
- 3 c. whole grain flour (Kamut®, spelt, oat, quinoa, farro, brown rice, etc.)
- 1/4 c. Rumford baking powder

Whisk all ingredients together, except baking powder, until well blended. Add baking powder last, whisking rapidly until mixed. Take out whisk and do not mix again. Gently ladle out of bowl onto a hot griddle.

Yield: 1 doz.
Prep. Time: 5–10 min.
Cooking Time: 2 min. each

Chef Brad tip

Rumford baking powder really gives pancakes a great rise. It is one of the secrets to multi-grain pancakes and waffles.

Five-Grain Pancake Mix

This is my idea of prepared foods—good-for-you food made in advance for fast and easy preparation.

6 c. wheat berries
1 c. barley
1 c. rye
1 c. oat groats
1 c. brown rice

4 c. powdered milk crystals
3 tsp. salt
1 c. Rumford baking powder

Mix grains together and mill into flour. Add remaining ingredients. Mix well. Store in freezer until needed.

Yield: 16 cups mix
Prep. Time: 10 min.
Cooking Time: Fast

To Make Pancakes:

Mix following ingredients together and cook on hot griddle.

1 c. pancake mix
1 egg, lightly beaten, or egg powder

1/2–3/4 c. water
1/4 c. sugar
2 Tbsp. oil

Multi-Grain Crepes

Any grain will work well for these. I love the flavor of the buckwheat. For a milder flavor, try Kamut® flour.

4 large eggs
1-1/2 c. milk
1 c. sorghum flour
1 c. whole buckwheat flour

1/4 tsp. salt
1/2 tsp. vanilla extract
1/2 tsp. xanthan gum
Touch of nutmeg
Your choice of filling

Grind sorghum and buckwheat on finest setting. Combine eggs and milk in blender. Add other ingredients and mix on high speed until smooth. Cook on nonstick skillet or with crepe maker. Fill with desired filling.

Yield: 2 doz.
Prep. Time: 10 min.
Cooking Time: 1 min. each

Chef Brad tip

Xanthan gum is a natural microorganism called Xanthomonas campestris. It is a great natural carbohydrate. It is a gluten substitute and is added to give volume to breads and other gluten-free foods.

For more information about ingredients and equipment, please check out Chef Brad's website, www.chefbrad.com, or email chef@chefbrad.com

Old-Fashioned Buckwheat Pancakes

Buckwheat brings back childhood memories. Nothing like a buckwheat pancake topped off with molasses.

    2-1/2 c. milk
    1-1/2 tsp. Saf-Instant® or other instant yeast
    2 Tbsp. molasses
    1-1/3 c. buckwheat flour
    1/2 c. cornmeal, finely ground
    1/2 tsp. salt
    2/3 c. high gluten bread flour

Between 8–12 hours before serving, scald milk and stir in molasses. Let mixture cool to lukewarm, then stir in yeast and let stand until yeast begins to bubble, about 10 minutes. Transfer to Bosch bowl. Using dough hook, stir buckwheat flour into molasses mixture. Stir in high gluten bread flour, cornmeal, and salt. Beat until smooth. Cover and let stand at room temperature 8–12 hours.

    1 tsp. sugar
    1 tsp. baking soda
    1/2 c. hot water (110 degrees)
    1 Tbsp. unsalted butter, melted
    2 egg yolks, lightly beaten
    3 egg whites

Just before serving, dissolve sugar and baking soda in hot water in small bowl. Stir this into prepared batter and then whisk in butter and egg yolks. Transfer mixture to large bowl. Beat egg whites in large bowl until stiff. Fold them into batter.

Breakfast Foods

Pour about 1/3 cup batter for each pancake on preheated griddle or into nonstick skillet. Cook over medium heat until bubbles form on top and underside is nicely browned, about 1 minute. Turn cake over and brown other side.

Yield: 18 pancakes
Prep. Time: Begin 8–12 hrs. before serving
Cooking Time: 2 min. each

Chef Brad tip

Recipes that call for scalded milk are usually old recipes that required scalding to kill bacteria. Today, unless you have raw milk, heating is adequate.

Halfway Blender Lemon Pancakes

My friend, Jason Porter, mentioned that he puts lemon in pancakes. I immediately went home and made some. Wow! I love the lemon flavor. Combined with the grains, it is a great way to start the day.

4 c. milk	3 eggs
2 c. whole grain (farro, barley, or spelt), cooked	1/4 c. oil
1 lemon, juiced and zested	1 c. high gluten bread flour or whole grain
2 Tbsp. powdered sugar	2 Tbsp. Rumford baking powder
2 tsp. salt	

Place milk and whole grain in blender. Blend for 3 minutes. Place in large bowl and add all remaining ingredients except baking powder. Whisk until well blended. Add baking powder and whisk again until incorporated. Do not mix again. Gently ladle onto hot griddle.

Yield: 2 doz.
Prep. Time: 8 min.
Cooking Time: 1–2 min. each

Chef Brad tip

Did you know that we need about 30 to 35 grams of fiber per day to experience better health and to prevent disease.

Super Fiber Blender Pancakes

Fiber should be the main concern for breakfast. I never knew fiber could taste so great.

2 c. water
1 c. soft white wheat
1 c. Super Fiber Blend (see page 81)

In blender, mix water, wheat, and Super Fiber Blend on high for 3 minutes.

1/4 c. buttermilk powder
1 egg
2 Tbsp. canola oil
3 Tbsp. pure maple syrup
1/2 tsp. sea salt

Blend 20 seconds more.

1 Tbsp. Rumford baking powder

Add Rumford baking powder, pulsing 3 times to mix in. Mixture will foam. Cook on hot nonstick griddle.

Yield: 26 3-inch pancakes
Prep. Time: 10 min.
Cooking Time: 2 min. each

Apple Blender Pancakes

Is this dessert for breakfast? Maybe these pancakes need a scoop of vanilla ice cream on top! This recipe is lactose free.

2 c. water
1/4 c. tofu drink mix
1 apple

1 c. pearled barley
1 c. oat groats

In blender mix above ingredients and blend on high for 3 minutes.

2 eggs
1/2 tsp. sea salt
2 Tbsp. canola oil

1 tsp. vanilla extract
Dash cinnamon

Add above ingredients and blend 20 seconds more.

1 Tbsp. Rumford baking powder

Add baking powder, pulsing 3 times to mix in. Mixture will foam. Cook on hot nonstick griddle. Dot with butter and drizzle with pure maple syrup for an absolutely scrumptious breakfast!

Yield: 26 3-inch pancakes
Prep. Time: 10 min.
Cooking Time: Minutes

Chef Brad tip

As they say, apples are really good for you—great fiber and lots of other great things. An apple a day, combined with lots of grains, will keep the doctor away.

Power House Blender Pancakes

Start your day out with these, and you will not be hungry for hours.

1/3 c. whole sorghum
1/3 c. whole buckwheat
1/3 c. whole Kamut®

1-2/3 c. water
1/4 c. dry powdered milk

Place above ingredients in Bosch blender and blend on high for 3 minutes with lid on.

1 egg
2 Tbsp. oil
2 Tbsp. honey

3/4 tsp. salt
1/2 tsp. xanthan gum
1 tsp. vanilla extract

After 3 minutes turn off blender, remove lid and add above ingredients, blending for 20 seconds.

1 Tbsp. Rumford baking powder

Remove lid, add Rumford baking powder, and pulse 3 times. Do not stir again. Gently pour batter out onto seasoned or nonstick surface. Flip over when pancakes start to show holes in top. Cook until done. Place on plate and immerse in melted butter and maple syrup.

Hot Corn Pancakes

Great for breakfast or as a side dish.

2 c. yellow corn grits
2 c. high gluten bread flour
1/2 c. brown sugar
1 tsp. salt
1/3 c. bacon grease or oil
1/3 c. tofu drink mix or powdered milk

4 c. water (or until desired consistency)
3 fresh eggs
1/4 c. Rumford baking powder

Mix all ingredients except baking powder until well blended. Now add baking powder and mix well. Don't mix again. Gently ladle onto hot griddle. Serve with gobs of butter and pure maple syrup.

Yield: 24 pancakes
Prep. Time: 5 min.
Cooking Time: 2 min. each

Chef Brad tip

Don't be afraid to use bacon grease once in a while. It really gives the food a real down-to-earth farm flavor— memories of Grandma's cooking. It was what she used.

Savory Kasha Corn Pancakes

Kasha is hulled, roasted buckwheat. This is a perfect gluten-free pancake.

- 2-1/2 c. kasha and corn flour, freshly ground (4 parts kasha to 2 parts popcorn)
- 2 c. water
- 3 eggs
- 1/4 c. red onion, chopped
- 1 Tbsp. Haco chicken base
- 3 Tbsp. peanut oil, cold pressed
- 2 Tbsp. Rumford baking powder

Whisk together flour, water, eggs, onion, base, and peanut oil. Whisk well and add baking powder. Whisk quickly and remove whisk from bowl. Do not stir again. Heat flat surface and gently ladle onto griddle, being careful not to stir batter. Cook until golden brown on both sides. Serve with applesauce, butter, maple syrup, or anything else that sounds good to you.

Yield: 1 doz.
Prep. Time: 10 min.
Cooking Time: 2–3 min. each

Those Wonderful Grains II

Potato Pancakes

Serve with maple syrup or applesauce. For the complete meal or side dish, these are perfect.

- 2 c. whole grain (farro, spelt, or barley), cooked
- 2 c. half & half
- 3 eggs
- 1/4 onion, finely chopped
- 2 medium potatoes, grated
- 1/4 c. oil
- 2 tsp. Rumford baking powder
- Salt and pepper

Place grains and half & half in blender and blend for 3 minutes. Place mixture in large bowl. Add remaining ingredients and mix well. In large skillet, heat about 1/4 inch of oil. Gently spoon batter onto hot oil. Fry until golden brown and turn over. Remove and place on paper towel to drain. Serve warm with applesauce or maple syrup and butter.

Yield: 1 doz.
Prep. Time: 10 min.
Cooking Time: 3 min. each

Chef Brad tip

Fried foods should not be a common occurrence at mealtime, but once in a while it tastes great and food is meant to be enjoyed in moderation.

Teff Kamut® Pancakes

Teff and Kamut®, the perfect combination for great pancakes. Teff gives waffles a crispy feel.

2 tsp. salt	3 c. Kamut® flour
1/4 c. tofu drink mix	1/2 c. teff
1/4 c. butter powder	4 c. water
1/4 c. vanilla instant pudding powder	1/4 c. Rumford baking powder
1/4 c. egg powder	

Combine all dry ingredients except baking powder. Mix well and whisk. Add water and mix again. Once everything is well mixed, add extra water if necessary. Add Rumford baking powder. Whisk well and let set. Do not stir again. Ladle batter on hot griddle without stirring. If you continue to stir, waffles or pancakes will be chewy.

Yield: 2 doz.
Prep. Time: 5–10 min.
Cooking Time: 2 min. each

Chef Brad tip

If you do not have butter powder, just use butter but double the amount.

Spelt Kamut® Pancakes

My wife thinks I make these pancakes with white flour. She cannot believe how light they are.

- 1 c. spelt flour, freshly ground
- 1 c. Kamut® flour, freshly ground
- 1 c. white spelt flour
- 1 tsp. salt
- 1/4 c. butter powder or 8 Tbsp. butter
- 1/3 c. tofu drink mix
- 1/3 c. instant vanilla pudding powder
- 1/4 c. Rumford baking powder
- 3 c. water
- 3 fresh eggs

Place all ingredients, except baking powder in Bosch bowl and whisk with wire whips until well blended. Add baking powder, whisk well, and let set. Do not stir again. Gently ladle batter onto hot griddle without stirring. Can also be cooked in a waffle iron.

Yield: 2 doz.
Prep. Time: 10 min.
Cooking Time: 2 min. each

Chef Brad tip

Spelt white flour is the equivalent of white flour, only it comes from spelt and is purer. A lovely flour if you are trying to get away from wheat.

Soft Wheat Pancakes

Soft white wheat is an excellent substitute for whole wheat in pancakes. It is so light and almost feathery.

> 2-1/2 c. milk
> 1/2 c. raisins or dried cranberries
>
> 2 c. soft white whole grain wheat

In blender mix above ingredients on high for 3 minutes. Stop blender and add following ingredients and blend for 20 seconds:

> 2 eggs
> 1/2 tsp. salt
> 2 Tbsp. oil
>
> 1 tsp. vanilla extract
> 1 tsp. cinnamon

After blending for the 20 seconds, stop blender and add:

> 1 Tbsp. Rumford baking powder

Pulse blender 3 times. Mixture will foam up. Cook on hot griddle.

Yield: 16 pancakes
Prep. Time: 5 min.
Cooking Time: 2 min. each

Chef Brad tip

> For lactose free, use soymilk or tofu drink mix in place of milk.

Kamut® Date Banana Pancakes

Kamut®, that totally wonderful grain, takes pancakes to a whole new realm—buttery and so digestible, These pancakes will delight you!

In Bosch blender add:

    1 c. loose dates
    3 c. water

Puree and add:

    1/3 c. tofu drink mix

Pour into Bosch bowl and add:

    2 c. Kamut® flour, freshly ground
    1 c. high gluten bread flour
    1 ripe banana
    1 tsp. salt
    1/3 c. oil
    1 c. sourdough starter

Mix until well blended. Add:

    1/4 c. Rumford baking powder

Mix again. Now let baking powder lift pancake batter. Do not mix again. Gently ladle batter onto hot griddle.

Yield: 2 doz.
Prep. Time: 5–10 min.
Cooking Time: 2 min. each

BREAKFAST FOODS

Amaranth Blender Pancakes

Amaranth, a super grain, really adds flavor and nutrition to these great blender pancakes.

1 banana	2 eggs
1/2 c. soft white wheat kernels	2 Tbsp. canola oil
	Dash nutmeg
1 c. amaranth flour	1/2 tsp. salt
1 c. milk, soymilk, or almond milk	2 tsp. Rumford baking powder
1 tsp. vanilla extract	

Place soft white wheat kernels in blender with milk. Blend for 3 minutes. Add remaining ingredients except baking powder to blender. Blend 1 minute. Add baking powder and pulse 3 times. Pour out onto hot griddle into small pancakes. Cook until top is bubbly, turn over, and cook until done.

Yield: 1 blender full of pancakes
Prep. Time: 5 min.
Cooking Time: Fast on a hot griddle

Chef Brad tip

There are no shortcuts to good health.

Yeasted Spelt Buttermilk Waffles

These are some of the lightest, tastiest waffles I have ever eaten! You won't even miss the white flour.

1 Tbsp. Saf-Instant® or other instant yeast
2 Tbsp. sugar
4 c. buttermilk
3/4 c. butter, melted
2 tsp. salt
5 c. spelt flour, freshly ground

This recipe works best if made up the night before. Place above ingredients in large bowl, mixing until all ingredients are well blended. Cover and place in refrigerator overnight. In the morning add following ingredients:

4 eggs, beaten
1-1/2 tsp. baking soda

Beat until well mixed. Prepare waffle iron by spraying cold iron with nonstick spray and heat until hot. Gently pour batter onto hot waffle iron and let cook until desired doneness is achieved.

Yield: 10 waffles
Prep. Time: Begin night before; 10 min. before serving
Cooking Time: 2–3 min. each

Multi-Grain Yeasted Buttermilk Waffles

These take a little more time to make, but they're worth it.

1 Tbsp. Saf-Instant® or other instant yeast	2 tsp. salt
2 Tbsp. sugar	1-1/2 tsp. baking soda
4 c. buttermilk	2-1/2 c. Kamut® flour
3/4 c. unsalted butter, melted	2-1/2 c. spelt flour
	4 eggs

The night before serving begin waffle batter. In Bosch bowl combine yeast, sugar, buttermilk, butter, salt, and flour. Use cookie whips to blend. Mix well. Place cover on Bosch and place in refrigerator overnight. Next day, when ready to serve, spray waffle iron with nonstick spray and heat up. Beat eggs and baking soda together. Whisk into batter until evenly incorporated. Ladle into waffle iron.

Substitution:
Exchange Kamut® and spelt flour for 5 cups of any flour.

Yield: 1 doz.
Prep. Time: Begin night before serving; 10 min. before serving
Cooking Time: 3 min. each

Chef Brad tip

About waffles...for a tender waffle, cook at a lower temperature. For a crisp waffle, cook at a higher temperature. To serve all at once, place cooked waffles in an oven preheated to 250 degrees. To store waffles, cool on wire rack and place in plastic freezer bags. Freeze up to one month.

Soft White Wheat Kamut® Pecan Waffles

Kamut®, the perfect grain for waffles—light and buttery and, don't forget, high in protein.

3 eggs	2 c. Kamut® flour
1/3 c. oil	1/4 c. Rumford baking powder
1/3 c. tofu drink mix	
2 tsp. salt	1 c. chopped pecans or hemp nut
4 c. water	
2 c. soft white wheat flour	

Preheat waffle iron. Whip eggs with oil in large mixing bowl. Add tofu drink mix, salt, and water. Whip until well blended. Add flours and whip until well blended. Add baking powder and whisk quickly, blending it well. Remove whip and do not touch again. Gently ladle batter out of bowl onto hot waffle iron, careful not to stir. Sprinkle with chopped pecans or hemp nut and close waffle iron. Cook until desired crispness. Remove from iron when done and cover with Peach Sauce (see page 104).

Prep. Time: 10 min.
Cooking Time: Minutes

Chef Brad tip

Waffles can be held in a 250-degree oven to keep crisp until served.

Ancient Incan Breakfast Cake

I love to imagine the ancient Incas eating food like this. Although they didn't have the modern conveniences we enjoy, I am sure they enjoyed their grains.

Mix in blender:

2 c. water	2 eggs
1/4 c. tofu drink mix	1/4 tsp. salt
2 Tbsp. oil	1 c. soft wheat, parched
1/4 c. brown sugar	1 c. amaranth, popped*

Add:

2 Tbsp. Rumford baking powder

Mix batter with 3 quick turns on high. Batter will rise. Pour into hot buttered skillet. Place on top rack of oven and bake until brown.

Yield: 8 servings
Prep. Time: 10 min.
Cooking Time: 12–15 min.

*For instructions on popping amaranth, see page 12.

Chef Brad tip

> Parched wheat is made by toasting the wheat in a dry, hot skillet until it is slightly popped and golden brown.

For more information about ingredients and equipment, please check out Chef Brad's website, www.chefbrad.com, or email chef@chefbrad.com

Peach Sauce

Better than syrup. If you don't have peaches, try fresh berries.

6 ripe peaches, peeled and chopped
3 c. water
1 c. sugar

1 tsp. vanilla extract
1/3 c. Ultra Gel or other thickening agent
1/2 c. butter (1 stick)

Bring water to boil and add sugar and vanilla. Dissolve sugar. Add Ultra Gel or other thickening agent to thicken. Add butter and peaches. Serve warm over pancakes or waffles.

Yield: 6 cups
Prep. Time: 5 min.
Cooking Time: 5 min.

Multi-Grain Breakfast Bread

Fills the basic needs for breakfast! It is wonderful, fast, and easy, as well as nutritious and sweet!

2 c. hot milk (110 degrees)
1 c. sourdough starter
3 eggs
2 c. your choice cooked grain or combination of cooked grains (farro, any quinoa, millet, or amaranth, etc.)
1 Tbsp. salt
1/2 c. butter (1 stick) softened

1 tsp. cinnamon
1/2 tsp. nutmeg
1 c. raisins
1 c. nuts, chopped
1/2 c. flax meal
6 c. high gluten bread flour or whole wheat flour, freshly ground
3 Tbsp. Saf-Instant® or other instant yeast

Preheat oven and pizza stone to 500 degrees. Place 2 cups cooked grain in Bosch bowl and mix with dough hook. Add milk, sourdough starter, eggs, salt, soft butter, cinnamon, nutmeg, raisins, flax meal, and nuts. Place half of the flour on top with yeast on top of the flour. Turn on Bosch and continue adding flour until dough pulls away from sides of bowl. Knead for 6 minutes.

Remove dough from bowl and divide into 3–4 equal parts. Roll each into 1/2-inch thick circles. Place on parchment paper. Let rise for 15–20 minutes.

After rising, if you like you can cut into strips. Twist strip then place back on parchment. Bake on hot pizza stone. If you do not cut into strips, bake like pizza on the stone. Both strips or bread bake in about 5–7 minutes. After baking, you can glaze with a maple glaze, if desired.

Maple Glaze:

   4 Tbsp. butter, melted
   2 tsp. maple extract
   4 c. powdered sugar
   1/4 c. milk or heavy cream

Whisk together until well blended. Drizzle over bread or twist. Eat and enjoy.

Yield: 3–4 breakfast breads
Prep. Time: 30 min. incl. rising
Cooking Time: 7 min.

Chef Brad tip

A pizza stone holds the heat so that baked goods not only come out better cooked but they cook faster.

Super Grain Breakfast Bread

Easy to make and so tasty. Nothing like waking up to the smell of freshly baked bread.

1-1/3 c. boiling water
1/3 c. teff
1/3 c. amaranth
1/3 c. white quinoa

In Bosch bowl add above grains, cover with boiling water, and let set for 10 minutes. Then add the following, except whole spelt flour, placing yeast on top:

4 Tbsp. butter
1/2 c. sugar
1 Tbsp. vanilla extract
2 tsp. salt
1 c. sourdough starter
1 c. hot water (110 degrees)
1 c. spelt white flour
1/2 c. sunflower seeds
1 c. dried cranberries
1 Tbsp. cinnamon
2–4 c. whole spelt flour
4 Tbsp. Saf-Instant® or other instant yeast
Topping: Butter, maple sugar, and pecans

Mix and continue adding whole spelt flour until dough pulls away from sides of bowl. Knead for 6 minutes. Next roll dough into two 10–12 inch circles. Let rise 10–15 minutes. Poke finger holes in dough. Brush with butter, maple sugar, and pecans. Bake at 475 degrees on pizza stone for 5–7 minutes.

Yield: 2
Prep. Time: 20–25 min. incl. rising
Cooking Time: 5–7 min.

Salads & Dressings

Life Just Got Better

That is what I decided when I found out how easy it was to add grains and beans to salads. It changed my whole life. My mission is to change your life in the same manner. You will be amazed at the wonderful taste sensations you will experience as you try out these recipes and create your own.

Some practical advice concerning using grains and beans in your salads: It works best if you prepare ahead. After years of encouraging people do this, with little success, it wasn't until I started teaching them to prepare ahead that instantly everything changed. They suddenly caught the vision. Cook up extra grains and have them chilled and in the refrigerator ready to toss in or on a salad.

It works! The same principle applies to beans as well. I have found that if you cook them and rinse them, they store extremely well and can be frozen, ready to use at a moment's notice. Grains and beans can be added to any recipe that you have. Any grain, any bean—it's just up to your taste. They add texture and flavor like nothing else.

Just a note on beans: There are so many different varieties. Heirloom beans, recently rediscovered by creative chefs, are now available, making cooking with beans exciting and tasty. Each bean has its own taste and texture. I love trying them out, and I have yet to find one that I do not enjoy. Pressure cooking has made it so easy, even in our busy lives, to add beans to our diet. Unsoaked beans can be cooked in under an hour and soaked beans can be done in about 20 minutes.

SUPER Super Grain Salad

Each of the grains adds a wonderful flavor and texture to this salad. Fresh mangoes would be great, also.

- 1/4 c. each, sweet brown rice, spelt, red quinoa, white quinoa, barley, bulgur, and Kamut®
- 1 each, red, yellow, and green bell pepper, diced
- 1 small red onion, diced
- 3 scallions, chopped
- 2 c. almonds, slivered
- 2 pkgs. dried mangoes, chopped
- 1 pkg. baked tofu, diced

Cook grains. Rice, red and white quinoa, bulgur, and pearled barley cook just like white rice. The spelt and Kamut® cook like brown rice. You can combine grains that have same cooking time (see page 36). Combine all ingredients in bowl with cooked grains and dressing and chill.

Dressing:

- 1/2 c. mango chutney
- 1/2 c. orange juice
- 1/4 c. Chinese plum sauce
- 1/4 c. sesame oil
- 1 Tbsp. ginger, grated
- 2 cloves garlic, crushed
- 1/2 tsp. black pepper

Mix all ingredients in blender until combined. Toss with grains and chill.

Marinated Beef & Millet Salad

Sometimes we just need to have a hearty, meaty salad. I usually serve this one with a lighter salad.

2 lb. stew meat
2 tsp. Spike
Balsamic vinegar

Brown meat with Spike in hot pressure cooker. Splash with balsamic vinegar. Close pressure lid and pressure for about 20 minutes on high, natural release. Remove from heat.

2 c. water
1 c. millet
2 tsp. beef base

Place all ingredients in pressure cooker and pressure on low for 7 minutes, natural release.

Marinade:

1/2 c. olive oil
1/3 c. flax oil
2 tsp. garam masala
1/4 c. balsamic vinegar

1/4 c. honey
2 fresh garlic cloves
1 onion, chopped

Toss meat and millet in prepared marinade and chill. Serve with fresh tomatoes and leaf lettuce.

SALADS & DRESSINGS

Pesto with Hemp Nut

Pesto is great on pizza, tossed with pasta or added to a pasta salad. It also keeps well in the fridge.

- 1 c. extra virgin olive oil
- 2–3 garlic cloves
- 1 c. hemp nut
- 2 Tbsp. lemon juice
- 1/4 tsp. sea salt
- 1 c. fresh basil leaves
- 3/4 c. pecorino Romano cheese, freshly grated

Place all ingredients in Bosch blender and mix until pureed.

Yield: 3 cups
Prep. Time: 5 min.
Cooking Time: None

Red Quinoa Onion Dip

Just one more way to add grains to your family's favorite dishes. This is a great chip dip.

- 8 oz. cream cheese
- 12 oz. sour cream
- 1 large red onion, finely chopped
- 1 c. red quinoa, cooked
- 1/4 c. amaranth, popped*
- Salt and pepper to taste

Place cream cheese and sour cream in bowl and whip until smooth. Add remaining ingredients and mix well. This recipe improves overnight.

Yield: 4 cups
Prep. Time: 5 min.
Cooking Time: 20 min. for grains

*For instructions on popping amaranth, see page 12.

Millet Fruit Salad

Perfect for breakfast! Make sure the grains are cooked tender. This should be light and fluffy.

2-1/2 c. millet	4 c. water
1/2 c. teff	1 tsp. salt

Place grains in hot boiling water and reduce heat. Simmer until done (about 20 minutes). Remove from pan and place in bowl and chill.

4 c. fruit, your choice (grapes, strawberries, pineapple, melons, etc.)	4 c. romaine lettuce, chopped (optional)
1/2 c. hemp nut	Dressing

Toss fruit with chilled grains and desired amount of dressing.

Dressing:

2 c. mixed fruit	1/4 c. orange juice concentrate
1/2 c. honey	
1/2 c. flax oil	Splash of balsamic vinegar

Place above ingredients in blender and blend well.

Chef Brad tip

> Hemp nut is perfect for adding those essential acids to your diet

SALADS & DRESSINGS

Pasta Grain Salad

Pasta and grains are the perfect combination. Add grains anytime to any pasta salad for a real treat.

- 3 c. pasta, cooked and chilled
- 2 c. farro, cooked and chilled
- 2 c. cannellini beans, cooked and chilled
- 1 handful fresh scallions, chopped
- 2 medium zucchini, chopped
- 3–6 tomatoes, chopped
- 2 c. almonds, slivered
- 1 c. feta cheese
- 1/2 c. amaranth, popped*
- Salt and pepper to taste

Combine ingredients.

*For instructions on popping amaranth, see page 12.

Dressing:

Choose 5 or 6 ingredients from your cupboard and create something exciting. Be adventuresome and do something a little different. Just have a little oil and vinegar on hand. Have fun with the other ingredients. Pasta salad can be exciting and fun. The biggest mistake people make is using cheap bottled vinegar, and the salad ends up without taste. If you choose to use cheap bottled dressing, at least dress it up a little with some good oil and balsamic vinegar. (If this all seems too difficult, just pick a dressing from one of the other recipes in this cookbook.)

Tomato Basil Bean Salad

Cool, refreshing, and packed with lots of great things for your body.

6 large tomatoes, cut into chunks
2 c. pink beans, cooked*
3 c. Kamut®, cooked*
1 large red onion
1 c. fresh basil, chopped
2 Tbsp. capers
1 head romaine lettuce, cleaned and chopped

Toss all ingredients in large bowl and set aside.

Dressing:

2/3 c. extra virgin olive oil
1/3 c. flax oil
1/2 c. balsamic vinegar
2 fresh garlic cloves
Salt and pepper to taste

Whisk together.

Yield: 24 servings
Prep. Time: 20 min.
Cooking Time: 45 min.

Chef Brad tip

Soak beans and Kamut® overnight. They can be pressured together for 20 minutes on high. Season with 1 teaspoon salt, 1/2 minced onion, and 2 pressed garlic cloves. Be careful not to overcook the beans. For the salad they need to be firm.

Sweet Potato Salad

Perfect side dish for a barbecue—or anything else, as far as that goes. Red quinoa dresses up any salad.

4 medium sweet potatoes	1/2 red onion, diced small
1/2 red bell pepper, seeded and diced small	4 Tbsp. parsley, finely chopped
1/2 green bell pepper, seeded and diced small	3 c. red quinoa, cooked

Peel and dice sweet potatoes in large pieces. Pressure for 3 minutes on low, quick release. Remove lid and place in ice water to chill for 1 minute. Add peppers, onions, red quinoa, and parsley.

Dressing:

3 Tbsp. Dijon mustard	1 Tbsp. Worcheshire sauce
3 Tbsp. ketchup	Juice of 1 lime or lemon
2 garlic cloves, minced	Splash of balsamic vinegar
3/4 c. extra virgin olive oil	Salt and fresh pepper to taste
3 Tbsp. red wine vinegar	

Whisk mustard, ketchup, and garlic together in bowl. Drizzle olive oil in slow steady stream. Add vinegars, Worcheshire sauce, and citrus juice. Mix well. Season with salt and pepper. Toss with potato mixture and enjoy.

Yield: 12 servings
Prep. Time: 20 min.
Cooking Time: 3 min.

Salmon Salad

Just another great way to use salmon.

1 c. millet
1 c. white rice
1 c. quinoa

Cook grains in chicken stock like you would white rice. Chill.

Salmon
Lemon pepper oil
Lemons, sliced

Cook, poach, or broil salmon, drizzled with lemon pepper oil with sliced lemons on top. Chill.

Dressing:

1 c. flax oil
1/2 c. olive oil
3/4 c. balsamic vinegar

1 red onion, chopped
2 Tbsp. dill weed
Salt and pepper to taste

Mix well.

Vegetables (chopped cucumbers, roasted red peppers, etc.)

Toasted pine nuts (optional)

Toss vegetables and grains together with about 1 cup dressing. In another bowl, toss salmon in about 1/2 cup dressing. Place grains on plate. Layer salmon next and drizzle remaining dressing over top. Add toasted pine nuts if desired.

Chilled Chinese Noodle Salad

This salad is wonderful to look at and even better to eat.

1 lb. fresh Chinese noodles	2 eggs, raw
2 c. quinoa (red, white, or black), cooked and chilled	4 oz. baked tofu
	2 tsp. sesame oil
1 Japanese cucumber	Red pickled ginger
9 oz. bean sprouts	

Cook noodles according to package directions. Drain and toss with sesame oil and set aside. Cut cucumber into julienne slices. Blanch bean sprouts. Make flat omelets with eggs and cut into strips. Cut tofu into julienne slices. Place noodles into wide, shallow bowl and arrange cucumber, quinoa, eggs, tofu, and sprouts in wagon wheel design on top of noodles. Place red pickle ginger in center of noodles. Pour dressing over creation.

Dressing:

1 c. dashi
1/4 c. sugar
6 Tbsp. rice vinegar
6 Tbsp. soy sauce
2 tsp. fresh ginger, grated

Heat all ingredients together until sugar dissolves and chill before serving.

Poached Salmon Salad with Avocado & Roasted Bell Pepper

It does not get any better. The avocado and roasted bell pepper are a perfect combination.

   2 lb. fresh salmon
   2–3 lemons, cut in slices
   Fresh spinach
   1/4 c. water

Place salmon on spinach greens. Place sliced lemons on top of salmon. Add water and poach for 20–30 minutes.

Dressing:
   1/2 c. flax oil
   1/2 c. balsamic vinegar
   2 tsp. dill weed

Mix. Toss salmon, crumbled, in dressing and pour over salad listed below:

   2 avocados
   2 roasted red bell peppers
      (canned), chopped
   2–3 lb. greens
   1 red onion, chopped
   Asparagus spears, steamed

Basil Bean Salad

Fresh basil adds delight to any salad. I think basil should be spelled f-r-e-s-h!

- 6 c. small white beans, cooked
- 4 c. farro, cooked
- 3 c. grape tomatoes, sliced
- 1 large onion, chopped
- 1 large zucchini, chopped
- 1 c. basil, chopped
- 6 c. romaine lettuce, chopped

Combine ingredients and toss.

Dressing:

- 1/2 c. olive oil
- 1/2 c. flax oil
- 2/3 c. balsamic vinegar
- 1 Tbsp. curry powder
- 1/4 c. honey
- 2 tsp. salt
- 2 tsp. lemon pepper

Blend all ingredients together and toss over salad.

Chef Brad tip

> Create a memory—
> take time to fix dinner
> tonight.

Farro & Bean Salad

Simplicity is really overlooked sometimes; we want to wow and amaze everyone. This one will do just that, and it is so simple.

- 6 c. beans, cooked
- 3 c. farro (or pearled barley), cooked
- 1 large red onion
- 2 c. broccoli, chopped with stems
- 2 c. raw carrots, shredded
- 2 c. tomatoes, chopped
- 3 Tbsp. fresh herbs, finely chopped

Mix all ingredients in large bowl.

Dressing:

- 1/2 c. balsamic vinegar
- 1/2 c. infused olive oil
- 1/4 c. Dijon mustard
- Juice of one lemon
- Salt and pepper to taste

Whisk together ingredients and toss with salad. Enjoy!

Kamut® Salmon Salad

With all the farm-raised salmon, we should be eating it more often. It is really wonderful fish if prepared right and fresh.

- 3 c. Kamut®
- 9 c. water
- 2 Tbsp. Haco vegetable base

Pressure for 1 hour on high, natural release.

Salads & Dressings

Salmon
Garlic oil

Plum vinegar

Brush cedar plank with oil. Brush salmon with garlic oil and plum vinegar. Bake 15 minutes on preheated cedar plank at 350 degrees.

1 c. grape tomatoes, quartered
1 c. kalamata olives, pitted

5 stalks asparagus, finely chopped
2 Tbsp. Spanish capers

Combine cooked Kamut® and salmon with above ingredients. Combine with dressing. Chill and serve.

Dressing:

3 cloves garlic
1/4 c. olive oil
1/3 c. flax oil
1/2 c. balsamic vinegar

1/4 c. plum vinegar
Juice of 2 lemons
1 tsp. sea salt

Whisk together ingredients. Combine with other ingredients. Chill and serve.

Chef Brad tip
> *Fish contains essential fatty acids. We need the good fat in our diets.*

Super Nutritious Summer Salad

This salad is packed with nutrition—very high in fiber and lots of important minerals and vitamins!

3 c. beans, cooked and rinsed
3 c. red or black quinoa, steamed
2 large heads leaf lettuce, washed and chopped
1 large red onion, chopped
2 large cucumbers, chopped
4 tomatoes, chopped
2 large carrots, grated
1 c. almonds, slivered

Combine all ingredients in large bowl and toss.

Dressing:

2/3 c. olive oil
1/3 c. balsamic vinegar
Salt and pepper

Mix ingredients. Pour dressing on salad and toss.

Fava Mixed Bean Salad

This is so good, make extra and feed some friends. They will know you like them when you feed them this!

2 c. fava beans

Soak overnight. Cover with water and pressure cook on high for 1/2 hour, quick release. Drain.

1 c. Colorado River Beans

Pressure on high for 1/2 hour, quick release, then drain.

- 3 Tbsp. red chili oil
- 2 c. pineapple, chopped
- 1 bunch green onion, chopped
- 1/2 can (12 oz.) stewed tomatoes
- 4 canned green chilies, chopped
- 1 bunch cilantro, chopped
- Salt to taste

Sauté onion, chilies, and pineapple in oil. Add tomatoes and cooked, drained beans. Sauté 2–3 minutes. Add cilantro and salt to taste. Serve hot as side dish.

Chilean Beet Salad

I really did go to Chile to get this recipe. I changed it only by adding the red quinoa. This salad is so pretty.

8–10 beets, cooked and cut into 1/2-inch pieces	3 c. red quinoa, cooked
8 eggs, hard boiled and chopped	Lemon juice from 2 lemons, freshly squeezed
1/2 onion, chopped	Mayonnaise, enough to make it nice

Combine ingredients and toss in large bowl. Season to taste.

Multi-Grain Potato Salad

This salad is the perfect example of adding grains to the simple dishes we already prepare for our families.

1/2 c. black quinoa	1-3/4 c. water
1/2 c. bulgur wheat	1 tsp. salt

Place grains in boiling salt water and pressure for 5 minutes on low. Remove from heat and let pressure fall naturally.

2 lb. red potatoes (do not cut or peel)

Place potatoes on trivet in pressure cooker and pressure for 7 minutes on low. Let pressure down naturally. While potatoes are still warm, cut into 1/4-inch squares and toss with 2 tablespoons white wine vinegar.

Salads & Dressings

1/2 c. red onion, chopped
1/2 c. sweet pickle relish
3 eggs, hard boiled
2 stalks celery, finely chopped
Mayonnaise Dressing (see below), enough to make it creamy
Salt and pepper to taste

Combine above ingredients with cooked potatoes and cooked grains.

Mayonnaise Dressing:

2 large egg yolks
1-1/2 c. olive oil (or corn oil)
2 tsp. white wine vinegar
3 tsp. lemon juice
1/2 tsp. Dijon mustard
1/2 tsp. salt
1 Tbsp. balsamic vinegar
Dash white pepper

Turn on blender. Add egg yolks and blend for about 15 seconds. Add all ingredients except oil. Blend well then add oil slowly, a few drops at a time, until emulsion forms. Continue adding rest of oil in a steady stream.

For more information about ingredients and equipment, please check out Chef Brad's website, www.chefbrad.com, or email chef@chefbrad.com

Kamut® Waldorf Salad

Simple salad made great by adding grains. Kamut® is wonderful in any salad.

5–6 apples, chopped
1 c. golden raisins
6 c. Kamut®, cooked

2–3 c. fruit cocktail, drained (reserve juice)
1 c. walnuts, chopped

Mix ingredients together.

Dressing:

Reserved juice
1 c. mayonnaise
1/4 c. lemon juice

1/4 c. flax oil
1/4 c. sugar
Dash salt

In separate container, mix dressing. Fold into dry ingredients. Chill and serve cold.

Sorghummus

Wonderful and nutritious—my version of hummus.

1 c. sorghum, cooked
3/4 c. water
Juice and zest of 1 lemon
3/4 tsp. salt
1/2 c. hemp nut

1/2 c. flax oil
1/4 c. extra virgin olive oil
2–3 fresh garlic cloves
1 oz. Parmesan Romano cheese

Place cooked sorghum and water in Bosch blender and blend for 3–4 minutes or until sorghum is well blended. Add remaining ingredients and blend until smooth. Place in refrigerator for 2–4 hours before serving.

Spanish Rice Grain Salad

A great way to use up the leftover Spanish rice.

8 c. Multi-Grain Spanish Rice (see recipe on page 166), cooked and chilled
2 heads romaine lettuce, cleaned and chopped
1 large red onion, chopped
3 large tomatoes, diced
2 large cucumbers, diced
2 c. cheese, shredded
2 c. beans, cooked and rinsed

Combine all ingredients in large bowl and toss with dressing.

Dressing:

1/2 c. olive oil
1/2 c. flax seed oil
2/3 c. balsamic vinegar
1 Tbsp. Mexican seasoning
1 c. salsa
2 tsp. salt

Combine all ingredients in bowl and whisk until oils and vinegar are blended well. Pour over salad and toss until salad is evenly coated.

Yield: 24 side dish servings
Prep. Time: 20 min.

Garbanzo Salad

The secret to good garbanzo beans is to overcook them a little. They become tender and tasty.

- 4 c. garbanzo beans, cooked
- 2 carrots, julienne
- 2 cucumbers, sliced
- 4 tomatoes, sliced
- 1/4 large red onion, thinly sliced
- 1/3 c. parsley, finely chopped
- 1 c. hemp nut
- 1/2 c. Parmesan Romano cheese, grated
- Fresh pepper

Combine and toss with dressing.

Dressing:

- 8 oz. plum vinegar
- 1 c. olive oil
- 1/2 c. flax oil
- 3 large garlic cloves, pressed
- 2 tsp. sea salt

Mix ingredients and toss with salad.

Multi-Grain Peachy Bread Salad

This salad is to die for! It has it all—taste, looks, texture, and perfection.

- 1 loaf of freshly baked whole wheat bread
- 1/2 c. butter (1 stick), melted
- 3/4 c. white sugar
- 2 Tbsp. cinnamon

Cut bread into chunks and toss in butter, cinnamon, and sugar. Bake in 325-degree oven until crisp.

1 c. rye berries
2 c. pearled barley
5-1/2 c. water

1 tsp. sea salt
4 Tbsp. butter, melted

Place in pressure cooker and pressure cook for 12 minutes on high, natural release. Remove grains and chill.

6 fresh peaches, diced
1 large cucumber, diced
1/2 c. golden raisins

2/3 c. pecans, chopped
8 oz. feta cheese

Combine chilled grains, toasted bread, fruits and vegetables, and feta. Toss with dressing. Serve right away. Enjoy!

Dressing:

1/2 c. extra virgin olive oil
1/2 c. flax oil
2 tsp. ginger powder
1 peach, pureed

2–4 Tbsp. honey
2 tsp. sea salt
Fresh parsley, chopped

Mix ingredients together.

Multi-Grain Bread Salad

A great way to use up bread. I prefer to use multi-grain bread in this recipe.

1 loaf of bread
1/4 c. rosemary or other infused oil
1/2 c. Parmesan cheese, grated
Salt and pepper to taste

Cut bread into chunks and toss in oil, Parmesan cheese, salt, and pepper. Bake in 325-degree oven until crisp.

1 c. rye berries
2 c. pearled barley
6 c. water
1 tsp. sea salt
1/4 c. olive oil
1/4 c. balsamic vinegar

Place in pressure cooker and pressure cook for 12 minutes on high, natural release. Remove grains and chill.

3 tomatoes, diced
1 large cucumber, diced
1/2 red onion, finely chopped
1 jar (7 oz.) kalamata olives, drained
8 oz. feta cheese

Combine chilled grains, toasted bread, vegetables, and feta, and toss with dressing. Serve right away. Enjoy!

Dressing:

1/2 c. extra virgin olive oil
1/2 c. flax oil
2/3 c. red wine vinegar
2 garlic cloves, crushed
2 tsp. sea salt
Fresh parsley, chopped

Whisk ingredients together.

Italian Bean & Grain Salad

So satisfying you might just want to eat it every day for breakfast, lunch, and dinner.

8 c. grains, steamed and cooled
8 c. beans, cooked, rinsed, and cooled
3 large zucchini, chopped
1 large red onion, chopped
1 c. broccoli, chopped
2 red bell peppers, seeded and chopped
6 tomatoes, chopped
1/4 c. fresh parsley, chopped

Add grains, beans, and vegetables together in large bowl.

Dressing:
1 c. olive oil
3/4 c. balsamic vinegar
1/4 c. pizza seasoning
1 tsp. pepper
2 tsp. kosher salt

Mix all ingredients together and toss with grains, beans, and vegetables. Chill and enjoy with a wonderful bread.

Yield: Not quite enough
Prep. Time: 10 min.
Cooking Time: 50 min. for beans and grains

Bulgur & Bean Salad

Light and refreshing, with just a hint of vanilla.

> 6 c. prepared bulgur wheat
> 3 c. prepared vanilla black beans
> 1/2 c. scallions, chopped
> 2 bell peppers, chopped
> 1/2 c. jicama, chopped
> 2 c. carrots, chopped
> 2 c. broccoli flowerets, chopped
> 1-1/2 c. walnut pieces

To prepare bulgur wheat, pour 3 cups hot water on 3 cups wheat and let set until water is absorbed. To prepare vanilla black beans, cook one part beans to 3 parts water, adding 1–2 inches of vanilla bean, finely chopped. Pressure on high for 45 minutes, quick release. Drain to use for salad. Combine ingredients.

Dressing:

> 1 c. olive oil
> 1/2 c. flax oil
> 1/2 c. plum vinegar
> 1 tsp. salt
> 1/2 tsp. pepper
> 2 cloves garlic, crushed

Mix ingredients. Toss with salad.

Fall Salad

Don't think you have to wait until the fall to enjoy this salad. Go to the produce market today and enjoy this salad tonight.

- 6 c. red quinoa, cooked
- 2 c. soft white wheat, cooked
- 1 red onion, chopped
- 1 portobello mushroom, chopped
- 4 c. grapes, halved
- 1/3 c. hemp nut
- 2 c. vegetables (zucchini, broccoli, squash, tomatoes, carrots, bell peppers, etc.), chopped
- 2 c. rice beans, cooked
- 1 Tbsp. pizza seasoning

Mix all ingredients in large bowl. Toss with olive oil and balsamic vinegar. Salt and pepper to taste.

Turkey Grain Salad

This is a great way to use up the leftover turkey. If you do not have turkey on hand, chicken works well.

- 3 c. turkey, cooked and chopped
- 1 c. red quinoa, cooked or 1 c. Kamut®, cooked
- 1 apple, chopped
- 1/2 c. golden raisins
- 1/2 c. almonds
- 1/3 red onion, chopped
- 1 tsp. white pepper
- 1/2 c. mayonnaise
- 2 Tbsp. mustard
- 1/2 c. sour cream

Mix all together. Salt to taste.

Vegetable Bean Salad

Great refreshing salad. Perfect nutrition for body and soul.

6 c. beans, your choice, cooked
4 large tomatoes, chopped
1 large red onion, chopped
1 green bell pepper, chopped
1 red bell pepper, chopped
1 c. kalamata olives
2 c. broccoli, steamed
8 c. romaine lettuce, chopped

Combine and toss.

Dressing:

1 c. olive oil (can replace half with flax oil)
2/3 c. white wine vinegar
1 Tbsp. mustard
1/4 c. parsley, minced
1/4 c. chives, minced
Salt and pepper to taste

Toss with vegetables, lettuce, and grains. Serve chilled as a side dish.

Yield: 20 small servings
Prep. Time: 15 min.
Cooking Time: 1 hr. for beans

Greek Fava Salad

Don't be afraid of those great big fava beans. If you can find fresh ones, use them instead.

4 c. fava beans

Soak overnight. Then cover with water and pressure on high for a half hour, quick release.

1 purple onion, chopped
3 oz. kalamata olives
8 oz. feta cheese, crumbled

Mix dressing and toss with beans, onion, olives, and cheese. Serve cold.

Dressing:

1/3 c. ginger vinegar
1/3 c. olive oil
1/3 c. flax oil

3 Tbsp. candied ginger, minced
2 cloves garlic, minced

Chef Brad tip

Instead of the fava beans, you can substitute with scarlet beans or mortgage lifter beans. These are extra large beans. We need the good fat we get from beans in our diet.

Beet & Kasha Salad

A little work but worth the effort. You will love the end result.

1 c. mayonnaise
1/4 c. Dijon mustard
2 Tbsp. bottled horseradish, well drained
Sea salt to taste
1 c. kasha, steamed
1/2 c. dill pickles, finely chopped
1/2 c. red onion, minced
1/4 c. fresh mint, finely chopped
2 c. yellow beets, cooked and diced
4 c. crisp lettuce, chopped
1/2 c. carrots, cooked and diced
1/2 c. sugar snap peas or snow peas, sliced
2 eggs, hard boiled, sliced
6–8 cherry tomatoes
Extra virgin olive oil
Herbed vinegar
Black pepper, freshly cracked

Whisk together mayonnaise, mustard, horseradish, and salt. Stir in kasha, pickles, onion, and mint. Mound kasha mixture in center of serving platter or on individual salad plates. Place chopped lettuce around edge. Arrange beets, carrots, peas, egg slices, and cherry tomatoes on lettuce. Drizzle olive oil and vinegar over vegetables. Sprinkle with black pepper.

Chef Brad tip

If you use red beets, assemble the salad within an hour of serving to avoid having the beets' color bleed, or substitute with rutabaga.

Salads & Dressings

Black Quinoa Pasta Salad

Don't be afraid to add other grains to pasta salads. This salad is best chilled.

6 c. pasta shells, cooked and chilled
2 c. black quinoa, cooked
1 c. red onion, chopped
1 c. celery, chopped
2 red apples, chopped
2 c. cheddar cheese, grated
1 tsp. salt
1/2 tsp. pepper
1-1/2 c. mayonnaise

Combine ingredients and chill.

Chef Brad tip

Black quinoa is high in lysine and really high in flavor. Cook quinoa like white rice, with a ratio of 2 parts water to 1 part quinoa.

Broccoli Salad

An old recipe with a new twist. The grains add a chewy quality and texture that is incredible. This is a crowd-pleaser!

- 8–10 pieces of bacon, crispy and crumbled
- 4 c. broccoli flowerets
- 1 c. whole grain (spelt, soft white wheat, or Kamut®), cooked
- 1 c. red grapes, halved
- 1 c. green grapes, halved
- 1/2 c. scallions, chopped
- 1/2 c. pecans, chopped

Mix broccoli, grapes, scallions, and cooked whole grain and chill. Add bacon and nuts. Toss in dressing before serving.

Dressing:

- 1 c. mayonnaises
- 3 Tbsp. apple cider vinegar
- 1/2 c. sugar
- 1/2 c. flax oil

Whisk together.

Yield: 24 side servings
Prep. Time: 20 min. not incl. cooking grains

Salads & Dressings

Pear Grain Salad

Green pears work well. They are crunchy and the dressing gives them a nice sweetness.

- 3 c. beans, cooked and chilled
- 4 c. farro, cooked and chilled
- 2 c. red quinoa, cooked and chilled
- 3 c. broccoli, steamed and chilled
- 4 large pears, seeded and chopped in 1/4-inch pieces
- 2 large heads of romaine lettuce, cleaned and cut in pieces
- 1/2 red onion, chopped
- 2–3 c. grapes, cut in half
- Salt to taste

Toss all ingredients together with dressing.

Dressing:

- 1 ripe pear
- 1/3 c. honey
- 2/3 c. olive oil
- 1/3 c. flax oil
- 2/3 c. red wine vinegar
- 1/2 bunch parsley
- 1/2 c. pineapple juice

Place all ingredients in blender and mix until pureed. Pour desired amount on salad and toss.

Yield: Large salad
Prep. Time: 15 min.

Chef Brad tip

> This is a great way to use the grains you have already prepared and have on hand in the refrigerator.

Red Quinoa Feta Salad

This salad is a flavor-rich experience, perfect for a special occasion or any occasion. This is red quinoa at its best.

6 c. red quinoa, steamed
1 lb. feta cheese
1 c. kalamata olives, pitted
2 roasted red bell peppers (canned)
1/2 c. olive oil
1 small red onion, chopped

2 garlic cloves, minced
1 Tbsp. balsamic vinegar
1 Tbsp. red wine vinegar
2 Tbsp. fresh thyme
Salt and pepper to taste
Juice from 2 lemons

In large bowl combine feta, olive, and roasted peppers. Add olive oil and toss lightly. Add onion, garlic, vinegars, thyme, salt, and pepper. Toss again. Add steamed quinoa and lemon juice. Toss and chill.

Yield: 12 large servings
Prep. Time: 10 min.
Cooking Time: 20–25 min. for grain

Chef Brad tip

Red quinoa cooks just like white rice, with a ratio of 2 parts water to 1 part quinoa. It can be cooked in a rice cooker, in a pressure cooker, or on the stovetop.

Vegetarian Taco Salad

Who needs meat in a taco salad when you add grains!

2 Tbsp. vegetable oil
1 onion, chopped
2 cloves garlic, chopped
3 Tbsp. chili powder
1 pkg. Yves Veggie Crumbles
2 c. grain, cooked
2 c. beans, cooked
1 c. vegetable stock, separated
1-1/2 Tbsp. cornstarch

1 head romaine lettuce
1 head iceberg lettuce
2 tomatoes, diced
2 c. cheddar cheese, shredded
1/2 c. black olives, sliced
4 scallions, chopped
1 avocado, diced
1 bag (14 oz.) tortilla chips, crushed

In hot oil sauté onion and garlic until soft. Add chili powder and cook 2 minutes. Add grain, beans, veggie crumbles, and 1/2 cup vegetable stock. Simmer 5 minutes. Thicken with cornstarch mixed with other 1/2 cup stock. In large bowl place chopped and cleaned lettuce. Add grain mixture on top. Add tomatoes, cheese, avocados, olives, scallions, and tortilla chips. Serve with dressing.

Low-Fat Dressing:

2 c. salsa
1 c. low fat mayonnaise (or regular)

1/2 c. low fat sour cream (or regular)

Blend salsa in blender until smooth. Add mayonnaise and sour cream. Serve with salad.

Holiday Mandarin Orange Grain Salad

Full of color and taste. Serve this with turkey or save for a side dish with those leftover turkey sandwiches.

8 c. grains, your choice (soft white wheat, barley, rye, oat groats, kasha, brown rice, Kamut®, etc.), cooked or steamed
4 c. mandarin oranges
2 c. dried cranberries
1 c. pumpkin seeds, toasted
2 c. pineapple tidbits
2 large cucumbers, chopped
8 c. romaine lettuce, chopped
1 large red onion, chopped

Cook grains and chill overnight. Add remaining ingredients and toss in dressing.

Dressing:

1 c. olive oil
3/4 c. balsamic vinegar
1/4 c. honey
1 tsp. salt
1 c. chutney
Dash cloves or cinnamon

Mix all ingredients together and toss with grains.

Yield: Enough
Prep. Time: 15 min.
Cooking Time: 20–50 min.

Soups, Stews, & Main Dishes

Just Do It

One of the best things I have emphasized in my cooking classes over the years regarding cooking with grains is to add them to everything that you cook. That is what I do. I add them to my family favorites with great results. I add grains to my Italian sauces, meatloaf and meatballs, casseroles, Mexican food, Chinese food, and anything else that I might be cooking. Grains add flavor and texture; they're also a great extender.

As I have mentioned before, it is easier if you have prepared and cooked up some grains in advance. They are then available to add at a moment's notice. It is easy and worth trying. I have tried every grain listed in this book in a soup and have loved it. I have sometimes used grains in place of beans and other times I have added both grains and beans to create very satisfying soups.

One of the keys to success in soup making is the quality of stock used as the base. Most soups that fall short of success do so because they lack taste. There is no excuse for bland, tasteless soups. There are so many ingredients available now, including a wide variety of wonderful grains, that add flavor and zest to food.

The key to using grains is just to do it. Just by adding grains alone to whatever you are cooking can increase your daily intake of fiber to a healthful range. Don't be afraid of tossing some into whatever you are cooking for dinner tonight.

If you need suggestions on adding grains to a particular recipe, email me at chef@chefbrad.com.

Fresh Sage & Portobello Mushroom Dressing

I personally love the contrast the black quinoa adds to this dressing but any grain would be great.

16 c. bread cubes	1 bundle fresh parsley
3 c. black quinoa or other grain, cooked	2 large onions
1 lb. bacon	6 eggs
6 stalks celery	4 c. milk
1/4 c. each, fresh sage, thyme, marjoram, and parsley	Turkey or chicken stock, enough to moisten
	2 lb. portobello mushrooms

Chop bacon. Place in skillet and cook until brown. Add celery and onions. Add mushrooms. Sauté until tender. Combine with all other ingredients, adding sufficient stock to moisten dressing, and bake at 350 degrees for 35–40 minutes.

Cooking Time: 35–40 min.

For more information about ingredients and equipment, please check out Chef Brad's website, www.chefbrad.com, or email chef@chefbrad.com

Chicken Noodle Soup

Chicken soup is meant to satisfy both the body and soul.

1 whole chicken
12 c. water
Salt and pepper

Combine and pressure for 15 minutes on high, quick release. Strain chicken stock. Reserving all liquid. Separate meat from bones. Return strained liquid and meat to pressure cooker. Add:

3 Tbsp. chicken bouillon	1 c. dehydrated green beans
1 c. Sofrito Herb Blend	1/2 c. dehydrated bell peppers
1 lb. egg noodles	1 c. whole amaranth or quinoa

Pressure mixture with meat and broth for 8 more minutes on high. Serve hot.

Sofrito Herb Blend

In blender or food processor, place following ingredients, blending well:

1 large onion	6 roma tomatoes
6 garlic cloves	2 Tbsp. dried oregano
1 bunch cilantro	1/2 c. olive oil
1/2 bunch parsley	1/4 c. balsamic vinegar
1 bunch scallions	2 Tbsp. pepper
2 jalapeños, seeded	2 Tbsp. real kosher salt

This can be stored in the freezer in small containers.

Spanish Tolosana Grain Soup

Each and every kind of bean has its own distinct flavor and texture.

1 c. Tolosana beans, soaked
1 c. whole grain (any kind)
6 c. water

Pressure beans and grain in water on high for about 25–30 minutes or until tender, quick or natural release.

1 large onion, chopped
1 large potato, peeled and cubed
1 large carrot, peeled and sliced
1 celery rib, sliced and cubed
1 heaping c. of green cabbage, sliced
1 large can (15 oz.) oven-roasted tomatoes in juice
Salt and pepper to taste

In pressure cooker sauté onion, potato, carrot, and celery. Add cabbage and tomatoes. Stir then add beans with liquid. Pressure on high for 5 minutes, quick or natural release. Salt and pepper to taste.

Yield: 8 servings
Prep. Time: 15–20 min.
Cooking Time: 45 min

Chef Brad tip

For optimal health you should eat at least six servings of beans each week—in everything from soups to salads. Beans are healthful and can be very tasty.

Creamy 9-Bean Soup

The combination of beans really makes this soup wonderful.

3 c. 9-bean soup mix	1 onion, chopped
2 cloves garlic	1/4 c. olive oil
15 c. liquid	1-1/2 lb. carrots, chopped
1 can (12 oz.) tomatoes, chopped, with juice	2 tsp. salt

Pressure all ingredients on high for 30 minutes, quick or natural release.

Hardy Rio Zape Bean Soup

Simple yet wonderful.

1/2 c. dehydrated onions	3 c. Rio Zape beans, sorted and washed
9 c. water	

Combine, pressure for one hour on high, quick release, then add:

8 oz. Demi Glaze Brown Sauce Mix	1/2 c. dehydrated mushrooms
1/2 c. tomato flakes	

Pressure for 8 more minutes. Serve hot.

Quinoa Spaetzle Dumpling Soup

Quinoa takes this recipe of simple dumplings from being great to fantastic.

3–4 qt. water
1 whole chicken
1 onion
1 garlic clove
1 bay leaf
1 celery stock

Combine all ingredients. Pressure for 30 minutes on high, natural release. Pour off stock and reserve. De-bone chicken and place back in stock. Place on stove and bring to boil. Drop spaetzle into soup. Serve hot.

Quinoa Spaetzle Dumpling Dough:

2 c. high gluten bread flour
1/4 c. quinoa flour
1/3 tsp. salt
2 eggs
1/2 c. milk
1/2 c. water
1/2 c. butter (1 stick)

Beat eggs lightly. Add milk and water. Place sifted flour and salt in bowl and gradually add egg mixture. The consistency of dough depends on type of spaetzle-maker used. Varying amount of flour used can change consistency. Also, increase or decrease amount of flour according to size of eggs.

Beef Barley Soup

It is no accident that beef barley soup is a comfort food. Barley is high in fiber and is a very satisfying grain.

1 c. rye
2 c. barley
5 c. water
1 tsp. salt

Bring water to boil and add grains and salt. Cover and simmer on low until grains are tender, about 45 minutes, or pressure for 14 min. on high, quick release.

1 lb. beef tips, cut up
2 c. portobello mushrooms, sliced
1 onion, chopped
3 garlic cloves
4 Tbsp. olive oil

Sauté in large pressure cooker beef, onions, garlic, and mushrooms until onions are tender.

3–4 qt. water
8 oz. Haco espagnole sauce mix
1/4 c. each, dried tomato and red bell peppers
2 c. cabbage, chopped
Fresh thyme
Salt and pepper to taste

Add above ingredients and cooked grains to sautéed beef tips in large pressure cooker and pressure for 10 minutes on high, quick or natural release.

Chalupa

Filling and satisfying at the same time.

1 c. whole grain (wheat, farro, spelt, or Kamut®), uncooked
3 c. Colorado River beans, uncooked
2 lb. stew meat or pork butt roast, cut into chunks
1/4 c. chili powder

1 large can (29 oz.) tomato sauce
1 large can (29 oz.) diced green chilies
12 c. water
1/3 c. Ultra Gel or other thickening agent
Salt and pepper

Brown meat in pressure cooker. Add remaining ingredients, except thickening agent, and pressure cook for one hour on high, quick release, then add Ultra Gel or other thickening agent to thicken.

Corn chips (Frito's)
Tomatoes
Avocados
Scallions

Cabbage
Green chilies
Cheese, shredded

Dice and chop vegetables. To serve place corn chips in soup bowl and top with soup. Top that with shredded cheese and vegetables. Enjoy.

Yield: 3 qt.
Prep. Time: 15 min.
Cooking Time: 1 hr.

Chef Brad tip

If a thicker soup is desired, add a little Ultra Gel to thicken it up.

Chili Verde

This is a classic Southwestern stew of pork and green chilies. Recipes range from really hot to mild—some so hot you cannot taste the food. I personally enjoy tasting the flavors of all the ingredients. Pressure cooking really brings out the flavors of this wonderful chili recipe. This recipe has won first-place ribbons.

3 lb. boneless pork butt
2 Tbsp. peanut oil
1 large onion, chopped
6 garlic cloves, minced
2 jalapeño chili peppers, stemmed and chopped
1 large can (29 oz.) green chilies, chopped
1/2 c. grain, your choice
1 tsp. oregano
2 lb. tomatillos
2 Tbsp. fresh cilantro, chopped
1 tsp. cumin seeds, toasted
2 c. beef broth
Thickener
Salt

Cut up pork into cubes, trimming off excess fat. Heat oil in large pressure cooker. Add onion, jalapeño peppers, oregano, and a dash of salt. Sauté for 5 minutes. Add pork and brown. Add green chilies, grain, tomatillos, broth, and toasted cumin seeds. Cover and pressure for 1 hour. Remove and thicken with desired thickener. Add freshly chopped cilantro and serve right away. Makes a great stew or filling for burritos.

Yield: 4 qt.
Prep. Time: 15 min.
Cooking Time: 1 hr.

Farro Chicken Stew

Better than barley, farro is so satisfying. Try this soup with the Red Pepper Farro Bread (see page 54).

2 boneless breast of chicken
1 onion
2 carrots, chopped
2 potatoes, chopped
4 c. farro, cooked
1/4 c. Haco chicken bouillon
Fresh parsley
Fresh garlic
2 cans (15 oz.) green beans
2 cans (15 oz.) stewed tomatoes
3 qt. water
1/4 c. olive oil
Salt and pepper to taste

Place chopped chicken breast in pressure cooker, sauté in oil for a couple of minutes. Add onion, carrots, potatoes, garlic, and stewed tomatoes. Place lid on pressure cooker and pressure for 8 minutes on high, quick release. Remove lid and add beans, farro, parsley, bouillon, water, salt, and pepper. Simmer to heat remaining vegetables.

Variation:

Chopped cabbage (about 3 cups would be great) is also wonderful in this recipe. It gives the stew a completely new taste.

Yield: 3 qt.
Prep. Time: 5 min.
Cooking Time: 15 min.

Chef Brad tip

Pressure cooking maximizes the results of stews and soups.

Arroz con Pollo

Chicken and Rice, or Chicken and Grains—however you say it, it tastes great.

2 boneless breast of chicken
1 (6 oz.) can tomato paste
2 tsp. oregano, toasted
1/4 c. capers
1/2 c. green olives, pitted
1 onion, diced
2 Tbsp. red wine vinegar
Cilantro and parsley, chopped
3 cloves garlic, minced
1 green bell pepper, chopped
Salt and pepper
3 Tbsp. sugar
1/4 c. peanut oil
1-1/4 c. each, white rice, quinoa, and millet
6 c. chicken broth

In large bowl place chicken, cut into pieces. Add tomato paste, oregano, capers, olives, onion, vinegar, parsley, cilantro, minced garlic, bell pepper, salt, and pepper. Mix together and set aside. In a large pressure cooker pan, place oil and sugar. When sugar is caramelized, add chicken mixture and place lid on pan for a moment. Cook for 5 minutes and add rice, or combination of grains, and liquid. Put lid on pressure cooker and pressure for 7 minutes on low, natural release. Serve with sliced onion and tomato.

British Isles Stew

I love stews on cold wintry days. Nothing tastes better, and barley is so satisfying.

- 1/2 c. pearled barley or farro (soak farro overnight with beans)
- 1/4 c. Haco vegetable base
- 3 c. soldier beans, soaked overnight
- 8 c. water

Combine and pressure for 20 minutes on high, quick release. Add:

- 1 c. carrots, chopped
- 1 whole onion, chopped
- 1/2 c. dried green beans
- 2 large potatoes, diced
- 2 cloves garlic
- 1/4 c. small white bean flour
- Splash of balsamic vinegar
- Salt and pepper to taste

Replace lid and pressure for 6 minutes on high, quick release, and serve.

Multi-Grain Meatballs

These can be made ahead of time and frozen.

- 2 lb. lean ground beef
- 4 eggs
- 4 c. oat groats/quinoa blend, cooked
- 2 tsp. garlic granules
- 1 tsp. black pepper
- 1/2 c. Parmesan cheese
- 1/2 onion, finely chopped
- 1 tsp. salt
- 1/4 c. red wine vinegar

Mix all ingredients until well blended. Form into 2-inch balls. Bake or drop in sauce and cook until done.

Potato Grain Bisque

What a wonderful bisque! This soup has body and excellent flavor.

In pressure cooker, place:

- 1 c. sorghum
- 1 c. buckwheat
- 4 c. potatoes, peeled and chopped
- 5 c. chicken stock

Pressure for 15 minutes on high. While that is pressuring, sauté in pan:

- 1 onion, chopped
- 4 cloves garlic, chopped
- 4 Tbsp. butter
- 4 Tbsp. olive oil

Sauté until tender. When grains and potatoes are done, add sautéed vegetables. Mix with wand blender, adding milk until smooth. Add:

- 2 Tbsp. balsamic vinegar
- Salt and pepper

Strain through fine-mesh strainer. Serve, topped with Crème Fresh.

Chef Brad tip

Crème Fresh is a wonderful Mexican-style sour cream, available at Mexican supermarkets.

Soups, Stews, & Main Dishes

Red Quinoa & Cabbage

Perfect combination—sweet red cabbage and the nutty flavor of red quinoa.

2 c. red quinoa, cooked
1 large head red cabbage
4 slices bacon, chopped
   (or 3 Tbsp. butter)
1/2 onion, finely chopped

2 apples, thinly sliced
1/2 tsp. caraway seed
1 tsp. salt
1/4 c. honey
1/4 c. red wine vinegar

Cut cabbage head into sections. Remove hard core, shred cabbage, and soak briefly in cold water. Chop bacon in small pieces and cook over low heat in saute pan until some of the bacon is crispy. Add onions and sauté until onions are tender. Lift cabbage from water, leaving it moist, and add to pan of cabbage and bacon. Place lid on pan and let simmer for 10 minutes. Add apples, caraway seeds, cooked red quinoa, salt, vinegar, and honey. Stir well and cover pan, allowing ingredients to soak up flavor. Serve as side dish with corned beef or pork.

Yield: 15 servings
Prep. Time: 15 min.
Cooking Time: 15 min.

Chef Brad tip

*Enjoy food more.
Make better choices in
the foods you eat.*

Kamut® Baked Beans

Kamut® is chewy and wonderful. Really adds extra flavor and health to this dish.

2 c. dry pink beans
2 c. Kamut®, uncooked

Add 9 cups water and pressure at high for 45 minutes, natural release.

1 lb. bacon, extra lean
1 onion, chopped

Chop and cook bacon until crisp. Add onion to crisp bacon and sauté until tender.

1 c. pineapple pieces
3 c. ketchup
1/2 c. molasses
1/4 c. Worcheshire sauce
1 Tbsp. balsamic vinegar

1 Tbsp. tabasco sauce
1 Tbsp. dry mustard
1 Tbsp. dry curry
1 tsp. kosher salt
1/2 c. brown sugar

Combine ingredients with beans, Kamut®, bacon, and onion. Bake in bean pot for 3-1/2 hours at 350 degrees.

Yield: 24 servings
Prep. Time: 25 min.
Cooking Time: 4 hrs.

Chiles Rellenos

I prefer this recipe because it yields a crisp, golden coating, especially good when made with polenta.

12 large green chilies, roasted
8 oz. Monterey jack cheese, cut into long narrow strips

Batter
Vegetable oil or lard

Roast chilies in oven until black. Place in plastic bag to sweat. Peel chilies, leaving stems on. Open small slit below stem and remove seeds if desired. Insert strips of cheese into chilies, using care not to split them. Place on paper towels to drain. Prepare batter (below). Preheat oil or lard to 375 degrees in electric skillet or nonstick fry pan. Dip stuffed chilies into batter and fry until golden. Deep-frying assures rounder looking chilies. Drain on absorbent paper towels.

Batter:

1 c. high gluten bread flour
1 tsp. Rumford baking powder
1/2 tsp. salt

3/4 c. yellow polenta or popcorn flour
1 c. milk
2 eggs, slightly beaten

Sift flour with baking powder and salt, then add polenta. Blend milk with slightly beaten eggs. Combine milk mixture with dry ingredients and blend together. (Sometimes more milk is needed to provide a smooth batter that clings to chilies.)

Yield: 1 doz. rellenos
Prep. Time: 10 min.
Cooking Time: 3–5 min.

Pineapple Quinoa Mexican Fiesta Salad

Straight from my Mexican/grain heart. Combine the two, Mexican and grains for a wonderful treat.

- 4 c. mortgage lifter and scarlet beans, cooked
- 4 c. grains (leftover Spanish-style rice), cooked
- 2 c. pineapple tidbits
- 1 red onion, chopped
- 1/2 c. red peppers, roasted and chopped
- 2 c. quinoa, cooked and chilled
- 1/2 c. pumpkin seeds, roasted
- 1 c. golden flax meal
- 1 large (1 lb.) bag tortilla chips
- 4 c. cheese (Colby cheddar or cheddar/Monterey jack blend), grated
- 8 c. romaine lettuce

Combine all ingredients into a large bowl and toss with dressing.

Dressing:

- 1 jar (16 oz.) salsa
- 1/2 c. olive oil
- 1/2 c. flax oil
- 1/2 c. balsamic vinegar
- 2 Tbsp. Mexican seasoning

Yield: 1 large salad
Prep. Time: 15 min.
Cooking Time: 1-1/2 hrs. for beans

Chef Brad tip

Mortgage lifter and scarlet beans are heirloom beans that, when cooked up, are the size of a grape.

South American Amaranth Pie

They probably have never heard of this in South America, but I liked the name and I love the pie.

4 c. water
2 c. whole grain amaranth

1 tsp. vegetable stock

Bring to a boil and then simmer for 20 minutes or until mixture is thickened. Next add:

3 small scallions, chopped
1/2 bell pepper, chopped
4 eggs

2 c. Colorado River Beans, cooked and drained
Cheese (topping)
Sour cream (topping)

Pour into nonstick pan. Cover with cheese and bake for 15–20 minutes at 350 degrees. Serve with sour cream.

Kamut® Millet Side Dish

So often we use rice and forget that there are a lot of other perfectly great grains that work just as well.

3 Tbsp. oil
1 Tbsp. sugar
3 c. raw millet
2 c. Kamut®, cooked
7 c. chicken stock

1 onion, chopped
2 garlic cloves
2 Tbsp. tomato bouillon
1/2 c. kalamata olives
2 Tbsp. pizza seasoning

Caramelize sugar in oil. Add millet and Kamut®. Toast. Combine rest of the ingredients in casserole-style pan and simmer until fluffy. Serve hot.

Turkey Meatballs Extra

I love the texture of the cooked sorghum and the fact that it is low in fat and tastes great!

In Bosch bowl with dough hook, place following ingredients and mix until well blended, 2–4 minutes:

1 lb. turkey meat, uncooked
2 c. sorghum, cooked (note instructions below for cooking)
1/2 c. hemp nut
2 c. multi-grain bread crumbs
6 eggs
1/2 c. onion, finely chopped
1/2 c. Parmesan cheese, grated
1/4 c. balsamic vinegar
2 tsp. garlic powder
1 tsp. salt
1 tsp. pepper

Combine ingredients. Mix until well blended. Form into balls. These balls can be frozen and used at a later date or cooked right away. To cook place 2 tablespoons olive oil in waffle-bottom pressure cooker and heat. Place meatballs in oil, browning slightly. You can stack the meatballs after you brown them.

4 c. tomato sauce
3 Tbsp. pizza seasoning

After you have browned the meatballs, cover with tomato sauce and sprinkle with pizza seasoning. Place lid on pressure cooker and pressure for 12 minutes for large meatballs, 8 minutes for smaller ones. Serve over pasta if you can wait for the noodles to cook. If you cannot wait, eat out of pressure cooker with a fork.

Yield: 2 doz. med. sized meatballs
Prep. Time: 20 min.
Cooking Time: 10–15 min.

To Cook Sorghum:

Cook in pressure cooker, using a ratio of 2 parts water to 1 part sorghum, for 15 minutes on low, natural release.

Fall Stew

To be enjoyed in the fall, winter, and even spring.

- 2 lb. stew meat
- 2 c. red quinoa, cooked
- 4 c. vegetables (zucchini, squash, carrots, broccoli, eggplant, etc.), chopped
- 1/3 c. parsley, freshly chopped
- 1 onion, chopped
- 1/4 c. roasted garlic olive oil
- 1/4 c. Haco beef base
- 1 c. soft white wheat, cooked
- 1/3 c. Ultra Gel or other thickening agent
- 8–10 c. water
- Salt and pepper to taste

Pressure meat for 30 minutes on high, natural release. While meat is pressuring, chop veggies and onion. Sauté in garlic oil. Add grains and sauté. Add beef base and water. Thicken with Ultra Gel or other thicking agent. Add beef.

Chef Brad tip

Good breads left to air-dry make great bread crumbs. I simply place them in a dry blender and in seconds I have wonderful bread crumbs.

Chicken & Rice Italiano

You will love this Italian-style version of rice and chicken. Be sure to add other grains. I would recommend millet and quinoa.

1 raw chicken	1 tsp. capers
1 can (6 oz.) tomato paste	1 c. tomatoes, freshly chopped
2 Tbsp. basil, freshly chopped	1 c. bell peppers, chopped
2 Tbsp. oregano, freshly chopped	1 c. onions, chopped
	1 c. mushroom, chopped
2 Tbsp. pizza seasoning	3/4 c. black olives, chopped

Cut chicken into pieces. Combine rest of ingredients and marinate chicken.

2 Tbsp. white sugar	3 Tbsp. oil
4 c. rice (or combination of rice and grains)	3 c. vegetable stock
	3 c. chicken stock

Carmelize sugar in oil and add marinated chicken. Sauté until brown. Add rice, or rice and grain combination, along with any remaining marinade, vegetable stock, or chicken stock. Pressure cook for 7 minutes on high, natural release.

Savory Lentil Meatballs

Light and tasty. So good you won't believe that they are good for you.

2 c. lentil beans, cooked
2 eggs
1 c. bread crumbs
1/2 c. raisins
2 c. oat flour
1 c. amaranth, popped*

1/2 c. carrots
1/2 c. broccoli
2 Tbsp. olive oil
4 c. tomato sauce
3 lb. lean ground beef
3 Tbsp. pizza seasoning

Place 2 eggs and raisins in food processor and blend. Add all ingredients except last three. Make a paste. Add ground beef and mix well. Form into balls and place on parchment paper. These will freeze well. To cook place 2–3 tablespoons of oil in bottom of pressure cooker. Heat to medium and place meatballs in oil. Cover with tomato sauce and sprinkle with seasoning. Place lid on pressure cooker and pressure cook for 12 minutes on high, quick release.

Yield: 4 doz.
Prep. Time: 20 min.
Cooking Time: 12 min. pressure cooker

*For instructions on popping amaranth, see page 12.

Chef Brad tip

A great way to get nutrition into your diet is to use beans as a base. Lentil beans cook up quickly in a pressure cooker or in a pan.

Multi-Grain Spanish Rice

Spanish rice is a treat any time, but now you have a wonderful treat that is healthful as well.

- 4 c. grains, your choice (my choice would be equal portions of white rice and red quinoa, uncooked)
- 1 small can (12-14 oz.) green chili enchilada sauce
- 6 c. beef, vegetable, or chicken broth
- 1 jar (16 oz.) salsa
- 1/2 c. pine nuts
- 1/2 c. pumpkin seeds
- 1/4 c. oil
- 1/4 c. sugar
- 2 Tbsp. tomato bouillon
- 1 Tbsp. onion powder

Heat oil in large kettle. Add sugar and heat until sugar starts to burn. Add grains, pumpkin seeds, and pine nuts, stirring regularly until well toasted. Add remaining ingredients. Bring to boil and reduce heat, simmering for about 20 minutes.

Yield: 24 servings
Prep. Time: 10 min.
Cooking Time: 20–25 min.

Chef Brad tip

> Any of the grains that cook like white rice can be substituted in rice recipes. Millet, all the quinoas, cracked Kamut®, oat groats, and hulled buckwheat all work well. I prefer to use a blend of grains with the white rice. In that way I get both the fluff of white rice and the nutrition of the whole grains.

Red Quinoa Coconut Yams

Festive and sweet, the perfect complement to any meal but especially nice for the holidays.

3 c. red quinoa, cooked
3 c. sweet potatoes or yams,
   cooked and mashed
1 c. sugar
1/2 c. milk

1/3 c. butter
2 eggs
1 tsp. vanilla
1/2 tsp. salt

Mix above ingredients, except red quinoa, and place in oven-proof pan. On top of yam mixture, spread red quinoa.

1 c. coconut
1 c. nuts, chopped
1 c. brown sugar

1/3 c. flour
1/3 c. butter, melted
Pinch of nutmeg

Melt butter. Stir in flour, sugar, nuts, coconut, and nutmeg. Mix until well blended. Place on top of quinoa and yam mixture like a crust and bake at 375 degrees for 35 minutes.

Yield: 12 servings
Prep. Time: 20 min.
Cooking Time: 35 min.

Super Grain Dressing

Try this one out with your roast turkey.

5 c. water	1 c. rice
2 Tbsp. Haco chicken base	1 c. millet
1 c. black quinoa	

Combine water and chicken base and bring to a boil. Add grains and cook like white rice.

6 slices bacon, cut and sautéed in 2 Tbsp. garlic oil until crispy	1 medium onion, finely chopped
3 loaves sourdough french-style bread, cut into small squares	1 c. mushrooms, finely chopped
1 c. celery, finely chopped	3 garlic cloves, finely chopped
	6 eggs

In large oven-safe bowl or large pan, combine above ingredients.

6 c. turkey stock
2 Tbsp. Haco herb seasoning
Fresh Romano cheese

Pour turkey stock over bread and vegetables. Stir in grains. Sprinkle Haco herb seasoning and grated fresh Romano cheese over the top. Cover with foil and bake at 350 degrees for 25 minutes. Remove foil for the last 5 minutes of baking.

Prep. Time: 25–30 min.
Cooking Time: 30 min.

Desserts

Enjoy

I am not a health fanatic. I love to eat, and I do love desserts. They are satisfying and, if nothing else, good for the soul. We live in a society of dessert-eaters. I have a family that loves dessert, so I decided to make the desserts a little more healthful by adding grains to them. I love to use the different flours when making cakes, sweet breads, cookies, and other treats. They have added flavors and textures that I have grown to love.

If we are eating properly, we do not need to feel guilty about eating desserts once in a while. If that is all we are eating, then we should feel guilty. Food, especially dessert, is meant to be enjoyed in all forms.

One of the greatest things about grains is the ability to grind them into flour. With all the grains available, we can substitute white flour and wheat flour quite successfully with great results, though most do not work like whole wheat flour. Many are light and produce great results in non-yeast baking products.

Don't be afraid to experiment with different grains in your baked goods.

Multi-Grain Cookies

These are soft and chewy. If you need chocolate, go ahead and add some.

1 c. butter (2 sticks)
1 c. brown sugar
1 c. white sugar
1 Tbsp. vanilla extract
2 eggs
2 c. oat groats flour

1 c. high gluten bread flour
2 c. quinoa and oat groats (combination), cooked
1 tsp. salt
1 tsp. soda

In Bosch with wire whips, cream butter and sugars. Add eggs and vanilla. Replace whips with dough hook and add flours, baking soda, and salt. Mix. Add cooked grains and mix until well blended. Spoon onto cookie sheet and flatten with hand. Bake at 325 degrees for 10–12 minutes.

Yield: 2 doz.
Prep. Time: 10 min.
Cooking Time: 10–12 min.

Chef Brad tip

> Chocolate may not be good for the body, but it is good for the soul.

Multi-Grain Cranberry Cookies

Super cookies—sweet but very satisfying.

2 c. boiling water
1/3 c. quinoa
1/3 c. millet

Several hours before making cookies, or the night before, cook grains (can be stored in refrigerator until ready to use). Boil water and then add grains. Bring back to boil, cover and simmer on low heat for approximately 20–30 minutes. Set aside.

1 c. butter (2 sticks)
1-1/2 c. fructose
1/2 c. barley malt syrup
4 egg whites
1 Tbsp. vanilla extract
3-1/2 c. spelt flour

1 tsp. salt
1 tsp. baking soda
1/2 tsp. cinnamon
3 c. of above cooked grains
1-1/2 c. dried cranberries
2 c. pecans, chopped

In Bosch bowl cream butter, fructose, and malt syrup. Blend in egg whites. Add dry ingredients, grains, vanilla, cinnamon, cranberries, and pecans. Dough will be more like a batter. Scoop onto parchment paper-lined cookie sheet. Bake at 350 degrees for 6–8 minutes.

Yield: About 4 doz.
Prep. Time: 15 min.
plus cooking time for grains
Cooking Time: 6–8 min.

DESSERTS

Rolled Barley & Carob Chip Cookies

Rolled barley is a great substitute for rolled oats, is higher in fiber and has a great taste.

2 c. high gluten bread flour
1 tsp. baking soda
1 tsp. Rumford baking powder
1/2 tsp. salt
1 c. unsalted butter (2 sticks), room temp.
1 c. granulated sugar
1 c. dark brown sugar, packed
4 egg whites
2 eggs yolks
1 tsp. vanilla extract
2 c. rolled barley
6 oz. carob chips
3/4 c. pecan halves, chopped

Preheat oven to 350 degrees. Line baking sheet with parchment paper. Sift flour, baking soda, salt, and baking powder together. Set aside. Cream butter and both sugars together. Add egg whites and egg yolks. Mix thoroughly. Stir in vanilla and then flour mixture. Mix well. Add rolled barley, carob chips, and nuts. Mix well after each addition. Drop by teaspoonfuls onto prepared baking sheets. Bake until golden, about 15 minutes.

Yield: 2 doz.
Prep. Time: 5–10 min.
Cooking Time: 15 min.

Chef Brad tip

Remember, it doesn't matter how healthful you make it, if your family won't eat it, you've wasted your time.

Multi-Grain Chocolate Chip Cookies

If you are going to make cookies, get creative and use different grains.

2 c. oat groats	1 c. white sugar
1/4 c. rye	1 c. brown sugar
1/4 c. sweet brown rice	2 eggs
1/4 c. millet	1 tsp. vanilla extract
1/4 c. amaranth	1 tsp. salt
1/4 c. quinoa	1 tsp. baking soda
1 c. butter (2 sticks)	2 c. chocolate chips

Place all grains into mill and grind into flour. Set aside. Cream butter, sugars, eggs, vanilla, salt, and baking soda in Bosch. Add flours and chocolate chips and mix until blended. Scoop out onto parchment-lined cookie sheets and bake in preheated 350-degree oven until golden brown, about 8 minutes.

Yield: 2 doz.
Prep. Time: 5–10 min.
Cooking Time: 8–10 min.

*For instructions on popping amaranth, see page 12.

Chef Brad tip

> We need to get out of the mindset that we have to use white flour in all of our baking. There are many grains that perform better and have more nutrition than white flour.

Kamut® & Barley Cookies

I love cookies, and I love grain cookies even better. I don't know if these cookies are healthful, but using the grains I feel better about eating them and feeding them to my family.

1 c. high gluten bread flour	2 large eggs
1 c. Kamut® flour	1 Tbsp. vanilla extract
1/2 tsp. salt	1 c. butter, room temp.
1 tsp. baking powder	1 c. granulated sugar
1 tsp. baking soda	1 c. dark brown sugar, packed
2 c. barley flakes (optional, replace with 1 c. popped amaranth* and 1 c. Kamut® flakes)	1 pkg. (6 oz.) semi-sweet chocolate chips
	3/4 c. pecan halves, chopped

Preheat oven to 350 degrees. Line baking sheet with parchment paper. Sift flours, salt, baking powder, and baking soda together. Set aside. Cream butter and both sugars together. Add eggs and mix thoroughly. Stir in vanilla and then flour mixture. Mix well. Add barley flakes, chocolate chips, and nuts. Mix well after each addition. Drop by teaspoonfuls onto prepared baking sheets. Bake until golden, about 15 minutes.

Yield: 2 doz.
Prep. Time: 10 min.
Cooking Time: 15 min.

*For instructions on popping amaranth, see page 12.

For more information about ingredients and equipment, please check out Chef Brad's website, www.chefbrad.com, or email chef@chefbrad.com

Quick Amaranth Cookies

Move aside oatmeal, we now have amaranth!

1 c. brown sugar, firmly packed	1 c. butter (2 sticks)
1 c. granulated sugar	2 eggs
	2 Tbsp. vanilla extract

Cream together the sugars and butter. Add eggs and vanilla and beat until smooth.

2 c. plus 2 Tbsp. high gluten bread flour	1 tsp. Rumford baking powder
1 tsp. baking soda	1 tsp. salt

Sift together and add to above mixture. When beaten smooth, add:

3 c. amaranth, popped*	1-1/2 c. chocolate chips (optional)
1 c. dried cranberries	

Beat the mixture well. Drop cookies 2 inches apart on well-greased cookie sheet and bake in preheated 350-degree oven until light brown, about 8–10 minutes.

Yield: About 3 doz.
Prep. Time: 8–10 min.

*For instructions on popping amaranth, see page 12.

Super Fiber Cookie Bars

My healthy friend and inspiration for many recipes, Jason Porter, loves these cookies.

2 c. butter, softened (4 sticks)
2 c. brown sugar
4 eggs
1 Tbsp. vanilla extract
5 c. soft white wheat flour

6 c. Super Fiber Blend (see page 81)
3 c. mini chocolate chips
2 tsp. baking soda
Dash salt

In mixing bowl blend together butter and sugar until creamy. Add eggs and vanilla, and cream again. Add baking soda, salt, and soft wheat flour. Mix well and add Super Fiber Blend and chocolate chips. Mix well. Place in large nonstick baking dish and pat smooth. Bake for 35 minutes at 350 degrees.

Yield: 2 doz.
Prep. Time: 10 min.
Cooking Time: 35 min.

Chef Brad tip

> Super Fiber Blend is my own personal blend, developed in a desperate effort to make a sort of healthful cookie.

Multi-Grain Shortbread

A classic, made better with grains.

1 c. butter (2 sticks)
1/2 c. sugar
1-1/2 c. flour
1/4 c. teff
3/4 c. amaranth, popped*

Cream butter and sugar. Add flour, teff, and amaranth and mix well. Form into 1-inch balls. Dust balls with flour. Stamp immediately with warm, oiled stamp. Bake at 350 degrees for 15–20 minutes.

Prep. Time: 25 min. incl. refrigeration
Cooking Time: 15–20 min.

*For instructions on popping amaranth, see page 12.

Chef Brad tip

The cookies will keep their shape better if refrigerated before baking. Chill 20 minutes on the cookie sheet after pressing.

Alegria (Happy Food)

This is a fun and very old recipe. You can find this treat in the markets in South America.

1/2 c. Karo syrup
1/2 c. honey
4 Tbsp. butter
1 tsp. vanilla extract
2 c. amaranth, popped*

Bring Karo, honey, butter, and vanilla to a boil. Turn heat down and boil for 10 minutes until golden brown. Stir in amaranth and pour onto nonstick permanent parchment. Cool and cut.

Crisp Topping

This is great on top of any pie filling or cobbler.

Lemon zest
1-1/2 c. brown sugar
1 c. rolled oats
1 c. spelt flour, freshly ground
1 c. amaranth, popped*
1/2 c. pecans, chopped
2/3 c. butter, melted
1/4 tsp. salt
1/4 tsp. baking soda
1/4 tsp. Rumford baking powder
Dash of nutmeg

Combine ingredients. Place over pie filling or cobbler and bake according to baking instructions for pie or cobbler.

*For instructions on popping amaranth, see page 12.

Bread & Butter Grain Pudding

Puddings in the pressure cooker are wonderfully moist and fast to prepare.

12 slices raisin cinnamon bread
2 c. cracked Kamut®, cooked
4 Tbsp. butter (plus 2 Tbsp. butter, melted)
3 large eggs
1/2 c. sugar
2 c. heavy cream
2 Tbsp. vanilla extract
1/2 tsp. nutmeg

Spray mold. Generously butter each side of bread. Stack into pudding mold. Mix remaining ingredients and pour over bread with 2 tablespoons melted butter. Pressure for 20 minutes in pressure cooker on high, natural release.

Lemon Sauce:

Juice of 1 lemon
Speck of lemon zest
1/2 c. sugar
1 c. water
1/4 c. Ultra Gel or other thickening agent

Blend ingredients together. Drizzle over cooked bread pudding while still warm.

Index

A

Alegria (Happy Food) 179
Amaranth 11,12,36-39, 43,48,53,56,57,60,61, 62,68,81,99,103,104, 106,111,113,146,161,165, 174,175,176,178,179
 Cooking tips 12,36,37
 History 11
 Nutrition 11,12,37
 To pop 12
 Uses 12,38,39
Amaranth Blender Pancakes 99
Amaranth Oat Dinner Rolls 62
Amaranth Olive Bread 53
Ancient Incan Breakfast Cake 103
Apple Blender Pancakes 90
Apple, Teff, & Triticale Bread 51
Arroz con Pollo 154

B

Baby foods 11,13,23
Barley 13,19,30,36-39, 64,78,84,88,90,94, 109,120,129,130,142, 150,153,155,173,175
 Cooking 36,37
 History 13
 Nutrition 13,37
 Uses 13,38,39
Basic Pancakes 83
Basil Bean Salad 119
Beans 3,6,108,120,122, 127,131,134,139,141,145, 148
 Black 66
 Cannellini 113
 Colorado River 123, 151,161
 Fava 123,135
 Garbanzo 128
 Heirloom 108,160
 History 11,17
 Lentils 165
 Mortgage lifter 135,160
 Nutrition 147
 Pink 114,158
 Rice 133
 Rio Zape 148
 Scarlet 135,160
 Small white 119,155
 Soldier 155
 Tolosana 147
 Uses 165
 Vanilla black 132
 White 119,155
Beef Barley Soup 150
Beet & Kasha Salad 136
Black Quinoa Pasta Salad 137
Blueberry Syrup 78
Bolillos 56
Bran 18,30
Bread & Butter Grain Pudding 180
Breads 41–72
 Amaranth Oat Dinner Rolls 62
 Amaranth Olive Bread 53
 Apple, Teff, & Triticale Bread 51
 Bolillos 56
 Brown Rice Spanish Bread 55
 Buckwheat Amaranth Rolls 60
 Buckwheat Feta Dough 63
 Cooking tips 38,42-44, 49,51,53
 Crispy Super Grain Pizza Dough 65
 Ethiopian Injera (Quick Method) 47
 Fruit Bread 51
 Granola Bread 46
 Hazelnut Multi-Grain Crackers 45
 Mango Amaranth Rolls 61
 Mango Banana Nut Bread 75
 Maple Glazed Fiber Rich Breakfast Bread 80
 Maple Quinoa Oat Bran Bread 44
 Multi-Grain Beehive Bread 48
 Multi-Grain Black Bean Pizza Dough 66
 Multi-Grain Bread Sticks 57
 Multi-Grain Breakfast Bread 104
 Multi-Grain Focaccia 70
 Old World Christmas Focaccia 72
 Popped Amaranth Focaccia & Pizza Dough 68
 Red Pepper Farro Bread 54
 Sourdough Kalamata French Bread 59
 Sourdough Sorghum & Buckwheat Pizza Dough 69
 Spelt Potato Nut Bread 52
 Spelt Sourdough Pizza 67
 Spelt Teff Focaccia 71
 Super Grain Bread 43
 Super Grain Breakfast Bread 106
 Sweet Teff French Bread 58
 Tender Pizza Dough 64
 Toasted Quinoa Cranberry Buttermilk Bread 50
 Zucchini Bread 51
Breakfast Foods 73–106
 Amaranth Blender Pancakes 99
 Ancient Incan Breakfast Cake 103
 Apple Blender Pancakes 90
 Basic Pancakes 83
 Blueberry Syrup 78
 Cranberry Buckwheat Muffins 76
 Five-Grain Pancake Mix 84
 Halfway Blender Lemon Pancakes 88
 Hot Corn Pancakes 92
 Kamut® Date Banana Pancakes 98
 Mango Banana Nut Bread 75
 Maple Glazed Fiber Rich Breakfast Bread 80
 Multi-Grain Breakfast Bread 104
 Multi-Grain Crepes 85

181

Those Wonderful Grains II

Multi-Grain Mango Coffee Cake 77
Multi-Grain Yeasted Buttermilk Waffles 101
Old-Fashioned Buckwheat Pancakes 86
Old-Fashioned Multi-Grain Granola 78
Peace Sauce 104
Potato Pancakes 94
Power House Blender Pancakes 91
Savory Kasha Corn Pancakes 93
Soft Wheat Pancakes 97
Soft White Wheat Kamut® Pecan Waffles 102
Spelt Kamut® Pancakes 96
Super Fiber Blender Pancakes 89
Super Grain Breakfast Bread 106
Super Grain Pineapple Banana Loaf 82
Teff Kamut® Pancakes 95
Yeasted Spelt Buttermilk Waffles 100
Zucchini Muffins 81
British Isles Stew 155
Broccoli Salad 138
Bromine 2
Brown Rice Spanish Bread 55
Buckwheat 36-39,43,45, 60,63,69,76,85,86,91, 93,156,166
Also see Kasha
Cooking tips 36,37
Nutrition 14,15,37
Uses 14,15,38,39
Buckwheat Amaranth Rolls 60
Buckwheat Feta Pizza Dough 63
Bulgur & Bean Salad 132
Bulgur wheat 66,69,109, 124,132
History 16
Nutrition 16,37
Uses 16,38,39
Buttermilk 50,51,76,77, 89,100,101

C

Cakes 12,17,20,39,170
Candies 11
Casseroles 27,29,33 (also see Main dishes)
Cereals 11,13,22,24,31,33 74
Chalupa 151
Cheese
  Cheddar 137,141,160
  Colby cheddar 160
  Feta 53,54,57,63,113, 129,130,135,140
  Monterey Jack 159,160
  Parmesan 130,146,162
  Parmesan Romano 45, 57,126,128
  Pecorino Romano 111
Chicken & Rice Italiano 164
Chicken Noodle Soup 146
Chilean Beet Salad 124
Chiles Rellenos 159
Chili Verde 152
Chilled Chinese Noodle Salad 117
Cookies 171-178
Corn 48,86,92,93
  Also see Popcorn
  History 11,17,22
  Uses 18,38,39
Crackers 31,45
Cranberry Buckwheat Muffins 76
Creamy 9-Bean Soup 148
Crème Fresh (about) 156
Crisp Topping 179
Crispy Super Grain Pizza Dough 65

D

Desserts 169–180
Alegria (Happy Food) 179
Bread & Butter Grain Pudding 180
Crisp Topping 179
Kamut® & Barley Cookies 175
Multi-Grain Chocolate Chip Cookies 174
Multi-Grain Cookies 171
Multi-Grain Cranberry Cookies 172
Multi-Grain Shortbread 178
Quick Amaranth Cookies 176
Rolled Barley & Carob Chip Cookies 173
Super Fiber Cookie Bars 177
Dough Easy (about) 67
Dough enhancer (about) 43

E-F

Egg Wash 59
Ethiopian Injera (Quick Method) 47
Fall Salad 133
Fall Stew 163
Farro 36-39,54,83,88,94, 104,113,119,120,139,151, 153,155
  Cooking tips 36,37
  History 19
  Nutrition 19,37
  Uses 19,38,39
Farro & Bean Salad 120
Farro Chicken Stew 153
Fava Mixed Bean Salad 123
Five-Grain Pancake Mix 84
Flax 78,81,104,160
Focaccias 68,70,71,72
Fresh Sage & Portobello Mushroom Dressing 145
Fruit
  Apples 51,90,126,133, 137,157
  Avocados 118,141,151
  Bananas 75,82,98,99
  Berries 51
  Blueberries 78
  Coconut 78,167
  Cranberries 50,72,76, 78,80,97,106,142,172, 176
  Dates 98
  Grapes 112,133,138,139
  Lemons 88,115,116, 118,120,121,124,126, 180
  Limes 115
  Mandarin oranges 142
  Mangoes 51,60,61,75, 77,109
  Melons 112
  Olives 53,57,59,121, 130,134,135,140,141, 154,161,164
  Peaches 104,129
  Pears 139
  Pineapple 82,112,123, 142,158,160
  Raisins 78,81,97,104, 126,129,133,165

Index

Strawberries 112
Fruit Bread 51

G-H-I-J
Garbanzo Salad 128
Gluten/gluten-free
 (about) 11,13,15,19,22,
 28,30,31,35,37,38,39,
 43,85,93
 (also see Wheat,
 Allergies/Sensitivity)
Grains Cooking Chart
 36,37
Grains Usage Chart
 38,39
Granola 46,78
Granola Bread 46
Greek Fava Salad 135
Halfway Blender
Lemon Pancakes 88
Hardy Rio Zape Bean
 Soup 148
Hazelnut Multi-Grain
 Crackers 45
Holiday Mandarin
 Orange Grain Salad 142
Hot Corn Pancakes 92
Injera 32,47
Instant vanilla pudding
 powder 96
Italian Bean & Grain
 Salad 131

K-L
Kamut® 20,21,36-39,70,
 77,81,83,91,95,96,98,
 101,102,109,114,120,126,
 133,138,142,151,158,161,
 166,175,180
Cooking tips 36,37
History 20
Nutrition 20,21,37
Uses 38,39
Kamut® & Barley Cookies
 175
Kamut® Baked Beans 158
Kamut® Date Banana
 Pancakes 98
Kamut® Millet Side Dish
 161
Kamut® Salmon Salad
 120
Kamut® Waldorf Salad
 126
Kasha 14-16,36-39,93,136,
 142
Also see Buckwheat
Cooking tips 36,37
Nutrition 15,16,37
Uses 15,16,38,39

M
Main dishes 21,33
 (also see Casseroles)
Mango Amaranth Rolls 61
Mango Banana Nut Bread
 75
Maple Glazed Fiber Rich
 Breakfast Bread 80
Maple Quinoa Oat Bran
 Bread 44
Marinated Beef & Millet
 Salad 110
Meats
 Bacon 72,92,138,145,
  157,158,168
 Beef 150
 Chicken 146,149,153,
  154,164
 Ground beef 155,165
 Pork butt roast 151,152
 Salmon 116,118,120
 Stew 110,151,163
 Substitutes 16,39
 Turkey 133,162
Millet 22,23,36-39,48,70,
 75,78,104,110,112,116,
 154,161,166,168,172,174
 Cooking tips 36,37
 History 22,23
 Nutrition 22,23,37
 Uses 22,38,39
Millet Fruit Salad 112
Multi-Grain Beehive
 Bread 48,49
Multi-Grain Black Bean
 Pizza Dough 66
Multi-Grain Bread Salad
 130
Multi-Grain Bread Sticks
 57
Multi-Grain Breakfast
 Bread 104
Multi-Grain Chocolate
 Chip Cookies 174
Multi-Grain Cookies 171
Multi-Grain Cranberry
 Cookies 172
Multi-Grain Crepes 85
Multi-Grain Focaccia 70
Multi-Grain Mango Coffee
 Cake 77
Multi-Grain Meatballs 155
Multi-Grain Peachy Bread
 Salad 128
Multi-Grain Potato Salad
 125
Multi-Grain Shortbread
 178
Multi-Grain Spanish Rice
 166

Multi-Grain Yeasted
 Buttermilk Waffles 101
Mushrooms 133,145,148,
 150,164,168

N
9-Bean Soup Mix 148
Non-yeasted breads 39,
Nuts 75,80-82,104,167
 Almonds 78,109,113,
  122,133
 Cashews 78
 Hazelnuts 45,82
 Hemp 52,102,111,112,
  126,128,133,162
 Pecans 77,78,102,129,
  138,172,173,175,179
 Pine 116,166
 Walnuts 126,132

O
Oat groats, see Oats
Oats 36-39,44,53,62,78,
 83,84,90,142,155,165,
 166,171,174,179
 Cooking tips 36,37
 History 23
 Nutrition 24,37
 Uses 24,38,39
Old World Christmas
 Focaccia 72
Old-Fashioned Buckwheat
 Pancakes 86
Old-Fashioned Multi-
 Grain Granola 78

P
Paellas 29
Pancakes/Waffles 6,14,19,
 20,33,35,38,74,83,84,
 86-104,144
Pasta Grain Salad 113
Pastas 19,31,35,111,113,
 137,163
Pastries 35,38
Peach Sauce 104
Pear Grain Salad 139
Pesto with Hemp Nut 111
Pilaf dishes 29
Pineapple Quinoa
 Mexican Fiesta Salad
 160
Pizza stones (about) 55,
 70,105
Pizzas 14,33,63-69,111
Poached Salmon Salad
 with Avocado &
 Roasted Bell Pepper 118
Polenta 22
Popcorn 17,18,93,159
 Also see Corn

183

Uses 38,39
Nutrition 17,18
Uses 17
Popped Amaranth
 Focaccia & Pizza Dough
 68
Potato Grain Bisque 156
Potato Pancakes 94
Power House Blender
 Pancakes 91
Pressure cooking 37,153
Puddings 17,33,180

Q
Quick Amaranth
 Cookies 176
Quinoa 36-39,57,70,75,
 78,83,104,116,117,146,
 149,154,155,164,171,
 172,174
 Also see Quinoa, black;
 Quinoa, red; Quinoa,
 white
 Cooking tips 27,36,37
 History 26
 Nutrition 26,27,37
 Uses 26,27
Quinoa, black 43,50,66,
 117,122,124,137,145,
 168
 Cooking tips 36,37
 Nutrition 26,37
 Uses 38,39
Quinoa, red 28,44,77,78,
 109,111,115,117,122,124,
 133,139,140,157,163,
 166,167
 Cooking tips 36,37
 History 28
 Nutrition 28,37
 Uses 28,38,39
Quinoa, white 26,106,
 109,117
 Cooking tips 36,37
 Nutrition 37
 Uses 38,39
Quinoa Spaetzle
 Dumpling Soup 149

R
Red Pepper Farro Bread
 54
Red Quinoa & Cabbage
 157
Red Quinoa Coconut
 Yams 167
Red Quinoa Feta Salad
 140
Red Quinoa Onion Dip
 111

Rice 16,19,22,26,29,
 35-39,75,109,116,127,
 154,160,164,166,168
 Cooking tips 36,37
 History 21
 Long grain, brown 29,
  36,39,54,55,70,83,84,
  133,142
 Nutrition 29,37
 Sweet brown, 109,174
 Substitutes 22,26,166
 Uses 28,38,39
 White 22-27,28,29,
  36-39,66,109,116,137,
  140,166,168
Rolled Barley & Carob
 Chip Cookies 173
Rumford baking powder
 (about) 83
Rye 36-39,64,84,129,130,
 142,150,174
 Cooking tips 36,37
 History 29
 Nutrition 29,30,34,37
 Uses 30,38,39

S
**Salads & Dressings
 107–142**
Basil Bean Salad 119
Beet & Kasha Salad
 136
Black Quinoa Pasta
 Salad 137
Broccoli Salad 138
Bulgur & Bean Salad
 132
Chilean Beet Salad 124
Chilled Chinese
 Noodle Salad 117
Fall Salad 133
Farro & Bean Salad
 120
Fava Mixed Bean
 Salad 123
Garbanzo Salad 128
Greek Fava Salad 135
Holiday Mandarin
 Orange Grain Salad
 142
Italian Bean & Grain
 Salad 131
Kamut® Salmon Salad
 120
Kamut® Waldorf
 Salad 126
Marinated Beef &
 Millet Salad 110
Millet Fruit Salad 112
Multi-Grain Bread
 Salad 130

Multi-Grain Peachy
 Bread Salad 128
Multi-Grain Potato
 Salad 125
Pasta Grain Salad 113
Pear Grain Salad 139
Pesto with Hemp Nut
 111
Pineapple Quinoa
 Mexican Fiesta Salad
 160
Poached Salmon Salad
 with Avocado &
 Roasted Bell Pepper
 118
Red Quinoa Feta Salad
 140
Red Quinoa Onion
 Dip 111
Salmon Salad 116
Sofrito Herb Blend 146
Sorghummus 126
Spanish Rice Grain
 Salad 127
Super Nutritious
 Summer Salad 122
Super SUPER Grain
 Salad 109
Sweet Potato Salad 115
Tomato Basil Bean
 Salad 114
Turkey Grain Salad
 133
Vegetable Bean Salad
 134
Vegetarian Taco Salad
 141
Salmon Salad 116
Sauces 12
Savory Kasha Corn
 Pancakes 93
Savory Lentil Meatballs
 165
Scalded milk (about) 87
Seeds
 Caraway 30,157
 Chia 81
 Cumin 152
 Flax 81
 Poppy 33
 Pumpkin 78,142,160,
  166
 Sunflower 78,106
 Sesame 48
Side dishes 15,20,25,92,
 161
Soft Wheat Pancakes 97
Soft White Wheat
 Kamut® Pecan
 Waffles 102

INDEX

Sorghum 43,45,69,85,91, 126,156,162
Sofrito Herb Blend 146
Sorghummus 126
Soups 13,15,21,28,33,38
Soups, Stews, & Main Dishes 143–168
  Arroz con Pollo 154
  Beef Barley Soup 150
  British Isles Stew 155
  Chalupa 151
  Chicken & Rice Italiano 164
  Chicken Noodle Soup 146
  Chiles Rellenos 159
  Chili Verde 152
  Creamy 9-Bean Soup 148
  Fall Stew 163
  Farro Chicken Stew 153
  Fresh Sage & Portobello Mushroom Dressing 145
  Hardy Rio Zape Bean Soup 148
  Kamut® Baked Beans 158
  Kamut® Millet Side Dish 161
  Multi-Grain Spanish Rice 166
  Multi-Grain Meatballs 155
  Pineapple Quinoa Mexican Fiesta Salad 160
  Potato Grain Bisque 156
  Quinoa Spaetzle Dumpling Soup 149
  Red Quinoa & Cabbage 157
  Red Quinoa Coconut Yams 167
  Savory Lentil Meatballs 165
  South American Amaranth Pie 161
  Spanish Tolosana Grain Soup 147
  Super Grain Dressing 168
  Turkey Meatballs Extra 162
Sourdough 46-48,53,54, 59,60,61,64,66-72,80, 98,104,106
Sourdough Kalamata French Bread 59

Sourdough Sorghum & Buckwheat Pizza Dough 69
South American Amaranth Pie 161
Soymilk 97,99
Spanish Rice Grain Salad 127
Spanish Tolosana Grain Soup 147
Spelt 31,36-39,42,46,52, 59,67,71,83,88,94,96, 100,101,106,109,138, 151,172
  Cooking tips 36,37
  History 31
  Nutrition 31,32,37
  Spelt white flour 52,59, 96
  Uses 31,38,39
Spelt Kamut® Pancakes 96
Spelt Potato Nut Bread 52
Spelt Sourdough Pizza 67
Spelt Teff Focaccia 71
Stir-fry dishes 33
Stuffings 29,145,168
Super Fiber Blend 80,81, 89,177
Super Fiber Blender Pancakes 89
Super Fiber Cookie Bars 177
Super Grain Bread 43
Super Grain Breakfast Bread 106
Super Grain Dressing 168
Super Grain Mix 43,65,82
Super Grain Pineapple Banana Loaf 82
Super Nutritious Summer Salad 122
Super SUPER Grain Salad 109
Sweet Potato Salad 115
Sweet Teff French Bread 58
Syrup, maple 44,89

T

Teff 33,36-39,43,47,48,51, 57,58,71,95,96,106,112, 178
  Cooking tips 33,34,36, 37
  History 33
  Nutrition 33,34,37
  Uses 33,34,38,39
Teff Kamut® Pancakes 95
Tender Pizza Dough 64

Those Wonderful Grains! 9-35
Toasted Quinoa Cranberry Buttermilk Bread 50
Tofu drink mix 64,67,83, 90,92,95,96,98,102,103
Tofu, baked 109,117
Tomato Basil Bean Salad 114
Triticale 34, 38,39,51
  History 33,34
  Nutrition 34
  Uses 38,39
Turkey Grain Salad 133
Turkey Meatballs Extra 162

U-V

Vanilla instant pudding powder 83,95
Vegetable Bean Salad 134
Vegetables
  Asparagus 118,121
  Bean sprouts 117
  Beets 124,136
  Bell peppers 109,115, 116,118,131,132,133, 134,140,146,154,160, 161,164
  Broccoli 120,131,132, 133,134,138,139,163, 165
  Cabbage 147,150,151, 157
  Capers 114,121,154,164
  Carrots 120,122,129,132, 133,136,147,148,153, 155,163,165
  Celery 125,137,145,147, 149,168
  Corn 48,86,92,93
    Also see Popcorn
    History 11,17,22
    Uses 18,38,39
  Cilantro 123,146,152, 154
  Cucumbers 116,122, 127,128,130,142
  Eggplant 14,163
  Garlic 109,110,111,114, 121,126,128,130,132, 135,140,141,146,148, 149,150,152-156,161, 168
  Green beans 146,153, 155
  Green chilies 123,151, 152,159
  Japanese, cucumbers 117

185

Jicama 132
Lettuce 136
  Iceberg 141
  Leaf 122
  Romaine 112,114,119,
    127,134,139,141,
    142,160
Onions 94,133,135,141,
  145-150,152,153,164,
  168
  Green 146
  Red 93,109,111,114,
    116-118,120,122,
    125,127,128,130,
    131-134,136,137,
    139,140,142,160
Parsley 131,139,145,
  146,153,154,163
Peas 136
Peppers 115
  Bell, green 109,115,
    133,135,140,146,
    155,162,164
    146,150
  Jalapeño 146,152
  Red peppers 54,160
Potatoes 22,52,94,124,
  147,153,155,156
Rutabaga 136
Scallions 109, 113,123,
  132,137,138,141,146,
  151,161
Shallots 72
Spinach 12,118
Squash 17,133,163
Sweet potatoes 115,167
Tomatillos 152
Tomatoes 110,113,114,
  119,120,121,122,127,
  128,130,131,133,134,
  136,141,146,164
Zucchini 51,81,113,119,
  131,133,134,163
Vegetarian Taco Salad
  141

W

Waffles, see Pancakes/
  waffles
Wheat 36-39,78,84,151
  Allergies/Sensitivity
    20,21,28,31 (also see
    Gluten/gluten free)
  Bulgur 16,36-39,66,
    109,124,132
  Cooking tips 36,37
  Cracked 60,61
  Durum 35,48
  Hard white 43,46,62,
    65,66
  History 22,31,35

Nutrition 35,37
Parched (about) 103
Soft white 75,89,97,99,
  102,103,133,138,142,
  163,177
Uses 35,38,39
Whole 44,50,55,70

X-Y-Z

Xanthan gum (about) 85
Yeasted Spelt Buttermilk
  Waffles 100
Yves Veggie Crumbles
  141
Zucchini Bread 51
Zucchini Muffins 81